a

haunted

love story

About the Author

Mark Spencer is the author of the novels *The Weary Motel,* *The Masked Demon,* and *Love and Reruns in Adams County,* as well as two collections of short stories and a history book about Monticello, Arkansas. Over 100 of his novellas, short stories, and articles have appeared in national and international magazines. His work has received the Faulkner Society Faulkner Award, the Omaha Prize for the Novel, The Patrick T. Bradshaw Book Award, the *Cairn* / St. Andrews Press Short Fiction Award, and four Special Mentions in *Pushcart Prize.* He and his wife, Rebecca, along with their three youngest children, have lived in the Allen House in Monticello, Arkansas, since 2007.

MARK SPENCER

a

haunted

love story

ၹၜ ၜၹ

The Ghosts of the Allen House

Llewellyn Publications
Woodbury, Minnesota

133.1
Sp34

First Edition
First Printing, 2012

Cover background texture © iStock.com/hudiemm,
Cover design and photo illustration by Kevin R. Brown
Cover photo © Rebecca Spencer, Rose © PhotoDisc
Editing by Sharon Leah
Interior photos © Rebecca Spencer

Llewellyn Publications is a registered trademark of Llewellyn Worldwide Ltd.

Library of Congress Cataloging-in-Publication Data
Spencer, Mark, 1956–
  A haunted love story : the ghosts of the Allen House / Mark Spencer. — 1st ed.
    p. cm.
  ISBN 978-0-7387-3073-8
1. Ghosts—Arkansas—Monticello. 2. Haunted houses—Arkansas—Monticello. I. Title.
  BF1472.U6S69 2012
  133.1'29767825—dc23
                        2011036071

Llewellyn Worldwide Ltd. does not participate in, endorse, or have any authority or responsibility concerning private business transactions between our authors and the public.
    All mail addressed to the author is forwarded, but the publisher cannot, unless specifically instructed by the author, give out an address or phone number.
    Any Internet references contained in this work are current at publication time, but the publisher cannot guarantee that a specific location will continue to be maintained. Please refer to the publisher's website for links to authors' websites and other sources.

Llewellyn Publications
A Division of Llewellyn Worldwide Ltd.
2143 Wooddale Drive
Woodbury, MN 55125-2989
www.llewellyn.com

Printed in the United States of America

Other Books by Mark Spencer

The Weary Motel

Love and Reruns in Adams County

Spying on Lovers

Wedlock

The Masked Demon

Images of America: Monticello

"Did you ever see a ghost walking?"
—PRENTISS HEMINGWAY SAVAGE IN A LETTER
TO LADELL ALLEN BONNER, NOVEMBER 8, 1948

හ ෙ

"The Allen House in Monticello, Arkansas, is a classic example of
what can happen when the spirits of the original owners
are intruded upon."
—*HAUNTED PLACES IN THE AMERICAN SOUTH,*
UNIVERSITY PRESS OF MISSISSIPPI, 2002

Contents

"IT'S HAUNTED, YOU KNOW"

The immediate response of the real-estate agent was, "Oh, you don't want that house."

In June 2005, Rebecca and I and our three children were new to Monticello in the southeast corner of Arkansas, where I had taken the position of Dean of the School of Arts and Humanities at the nearby university. We were living in a cramped rental house with crooked floors, and we had just asked about buying the house at 705 North Main Street.

The real-estate agent, who had been all smiles when we first walked into her office, frowned and stood up from her desk. She shook her head and said, "I got an old two-story stucco on South Main if you want to see something else." She sat back down behind her big desk, and looking at some papers lying on the ink blotter, "Just take my word for it honey. You don't want that house." The pleasant lilt in her Arkansas accent was gone.

So much for Southern hospitality, I thought.

Rebecca leaned over the woman's desk a little, smiled, and said, "Oh, but I do want that house. We love that house, and we want you to approach the owner to see if she'll consider an offer."

The agent picked up a pen and started writing on the papers before her. "Nope. No can do, folks." She didn't look up again. Rebecca and I had been dismissed. We looked at each other, dumbfounded. We had apparently moved to a town where real-estate agents cared little about earning commissions.

Another agent in the small office, a bald man with large sad eyes, cleared his throat. He pressed his lips together nervously. "Well, let's just say—" he began. Then he stood up from his desk. He shifted his weight from one foot to the other while looking out a window. He stuck his hands in his pants pockets. Finally, still looking out the window, he said, "Well, let's just say that the house has a history."

We looked at each other and immediately decided to take a different approach to contacting the owner. We would simply go to the house and knock on the front door and introduce ourselves.

৵৹ ৹৵

Two months earlier, Rebecca had come to town with me for my job interview, and as soon as we had arrived, we circled the quaint town square and drove down Main Street to get a sense of the place. We drove slowly, admiring all the big century-old houses with their white columns, second-story sleeping porches, gingerbread woodwork, and widow's walks. Then we came to a stunning Victorian mansion. I stopped the car in the middle of the street and we gawked.

It had a three-story octagonal turret on one end, a four-story round turret on the other, and spires rising from the towers. A massive portico was supported by clusters of Corinthian columns. Large stained-glass windows framed the front door. The house was rather rundown but gorgeous nonetheless.

Rebecca said, "I'll move to this town if you buy me that house."

There was no for-sale sign in the yard. "But it doesn't appear to be for sale," I said.

Rebecca shook her head. "I don't care. I will make it happen."

The Allen House 2005

Whenever Rebecca says she will make something happen, I look at her and my right eyebrow rises, revealing my skepticism. Her grandmother was a witch, and Rebecca has made the claim that such an attribute can be inherited.

∾ ౷

We pulled into the driveway of 705 North Main Street. Actually, we *crept shyly* into the driveway, because we had no idea how the owner would react to strangers appearing at her door and announcing that they coveted her house and wanted to buy it. We knew a woman lived there alone, but we knew nothing about her.

From the driveway, the sad condition of the mansion was more evident. Much of the house wasn't visible from the street because of the untrimmed bushes and large magnolia trees. Now I could see how ivy climbed unchecked up the huge Corinthian columns all the way to the portico roof, where its lush tendrils spilled over the stanchions and railings. Old paint curled away from the eaves and flaked from window casings. The wrought-iron railing on the widow's walk was rusted. Some of the tin roof tiles looked dented. Rust from the old nails had bled down the clapboards. The huge trees cast gloomy shadows over the house, and blotches of black mold grew thick as beards under window sills. The wooden railings on top of the portico were rotted, and some of the window panes were cracked.

I began to have second thoughts about buying this place. I was having second thoughts about even knocking on the front door. I think Rebecca was too because she said, "I'll stay in the car. It'll be better if just you go."

Next to the garage, a white 1955 Thunderbird covered with a thick layer of dust was parked cock-eyed. Next to it was a 1972 Mercedes 450 SL with a flat tire. The open two-car garage was empty.

I said, "I don't think she's home."

"Go see."

"Okay, but what am I going to say?"

"Just start by saying you're a new dean at the university and you love the house."

I stepped out of the car, and something scurried through the high grass. A blue jay in a magnolia tree eyed me as I approached the house. Flower beds near the porch were choked with weeds. Old rose bushes sprawled. The wooden steps screeched under my weight. On the wooden porch, I stepped gingerly and anticipated falling through. I thought, *Jeez, this place would make a great haunted house.* I wouldn't have been surprised to see a coffin.

A man's voice came from inside the house. Full of the peaks and hollows of the Ozark hills, the voice spewed anger and horror. I got chills. Then I realized that it was a radio evangelist warning his listeners at two o'clock on a weekday afternoon of the terrors of Hell.

I rang the doorbell, and a series of loud chimes reverberated through the house. I hoped no one was at home, but I waited. In the cobwebs above my head, a spider was slowly consuming a fly.

The radio preacher ranted, "And you shall be cast into the fiery pit!" No other sound came from the house.

Back in the car, I said, "This place is in bad shape. Real bad shape."

Rebecca said, "Good. We can get it cheap."

"Maybe. We'll have to think about it," I said as I backed the car out of the driveway. "The place is a real wreck."

"Pull up to the curb. I want to look at it some more," Rebecca said.

I did as she asked. The house was on her side of the car. While she looked at the wreck, I noticed the old but well-kept house across the street. I admired the nicely trimmed yard and what looked like a fresh paint job. *That is what we need*, I said to myself. I was about to say so to Rebecca, but when I looked over at her and saw the way she was gazing at the rundown Victorian, I looked up at it myself. From the street, it again appealed to me the way it had the first time I saw it. Massive and convoluted, but also elegant. It was a lovely ruin, rich in character, and in desperate need of care.

Rebecca was apparently thinking the same thing I was. She said, "It needs us."

A couple of weeks later, I would drive past the house with an out-of-town visitor and say, "What do you think?"

He smirked and said, "Looks like there oughta be a coffin on the front porch."

∽ ∾

We let all our new friends and acquaintances in Monticello know we were interested in the big Victorian on North Main.

"Oh, it's called the Allen House," someone soon told us. "You don't want to buy that house. It ought to be torn down."

We asked about the owner.

One person told us, "She'll never sell it. People have tried to buy it from her, but she won't even talk about it."

Lots of people said we were pipe dreaming. We'd never get the house they assured us. People had tried before, but the woman had moved to Monticello years ago just to live in that house.

An elderly lady, a life-long resident of the town, said, "I know her vaguely. Name's Mona or Margaret or Myrtle. Something with an 'M.' I see her in Piggly Wiggly once in a while buying her groceries. She likes carrots. Always has lots of carrots. Don't see her often, though. She's gone a lot on trips. Travels all over the world is what I understand. You can't miss her if you ever see her. She's very beautiful."

I said, "Well, next time you see her at the Piggly Wiggly, let her know we want to buy her house."

"Oh, she'll never sell it. Besides, it's haunted, you know."

Almost every time Rebecca and I mentioned to someone that we wanted to buy the Allen House, the inevitable response was, "It's haunted, you know." Seldom did anyone say, "People *say* it's haunted," or, "It's *supposed* to be haunted." People usually stated flatly, "It's haunted, you know."

∽๑ ๑∾

I did an Internet search for "Allen House, Monticello, Arkansas," and sure enough, the hits I got were all about the house's history of paranormal activity. Built in 1906, the house reportedly became haunted in the 1940s after Ladell Allen Bonner, the middle of three daughters of entrepreneur Joe Lee Allen and his wife Caddye, took poison in the master-bedroom suite, which was subsequently sealed by Ladell's mother as a memorial to her daughter. When it was finally opened more than thirty-five years later, the poison was found on a closet shelf.

Some of the articles mentioned Ladell's son, Allen Bonner, as another ghost in the house.

The standard narrative about the house was that it served as apartments from the mid-1950s to the mid-1980s. Tenants had on occasion been so convinced of the presence of intruders in the attic that the police were called ... to find nothing. In addition, some of the tenants were so frightened by sounds and small items being unexplainably moved that they lived in the house only a short time. For one tenant, the day some of his heavy furniture got moved around was the day he had had enough, and he vacated the house immediately.

A college student in 1968 took a photo of his new bride in the dining room, and when the photo was developed, it revealed a ghostly figure of a woman hovering in the room.

The Internet articles also mentioned Carolyn Wilson, a resident in 1959, who was inspired by the house to write her popular 1966 Gothic romance *The Scent of Lilacs,* in which a young newlywed finds herself living in an old mansion that appears to be haunted.

As for other instances of paranormal activity in the Allen House, the articles told of a female guest at a party who claimed to get trapped in the downstairs bathroom by a ghost. After struggling with the door for several minutes, she was suddenly able to swing it open without effort.

Thinking a friend of theirs was playing a trick on them and hiding in a closet, a couple held the door shut against a force pushing from inside. Then the friend who they assumed was in the closet walked into their apartment and asked what they were doing. Startled and confused, the couple immediately opened the closet door to find … nothing.

Not only was the main house supposed to be haunted but the carriage house had been the site of paranormal activity as well. Throughout the 1960s and 70s, tenants in the carriage house were difficult to retain because of objects being moved around and the unmistakable sound of human moaning.

When the house passed to new owners in the mid-1980s, a servant claimed that one morning as she was going up the stairs "Miss Ladell" was coming down. The servant left and refused to return. When the owners set up a gift shop in the back of the house in the early 1990s, objects got moved over night and mysteriously broken.

There were also stories of decorative swords flying off of walls, of a former owner coming downstairs one morning to find three ghostly little girls playing in the foyer, and of Ladell Allen Bonner crying in the night.

When I showed the write-ups to Rebecca, she read them with interest. Then she shrugged and said she wasn't scared off from trying to buy the house. "So what?" she said. I agreed. In fact, I was inclined to believe the stories were all fabrications of over-active imaginations.

᳗ Chapter 2 ᳝

MARILYN MONROE AT SIXTY

The name of the woman we bought the Allen House from is not really "Marilyn," but that's what I'll call her. One reason I chose this name is that the first time I laid eyes on her—under the muted light of a sparkling chandelier in the foyer of the Allen House—it was like meeting an apparition of Marilyn Monroe. She was certainly not the gnarly crone I had imagined she would be that first time I stood on her porch. This woman had an hour-glass figure, big Texas-style blonde hair, a breathy and child-like voice. She was nearly sixty years old, but in the dim light she could have passed for thirty-five.

In July 2005, word had reached Marilyn that some new people in town wanted her house. She had called me at my office at the university. With her breathy voice, she sounded rather charming. She asked about me and my wife and our small boys and our daughter, Brontë, who was nine. She seemed enthusiastic about our having a little girl and said, "Oh, she would feel like a princess in the house. An absolute princess!" Contrary to what everybody in town had told us, she said she might consider selling.

Rebecca and I were very excited and arranged to see the inside of the house one evening as soon as Marilyn returned home from a shopping trip to Dallas.

While we waited for the appointed evening, we drove past the house frequently. In part, this was because we looked for reasons to get out of our cramped rental house with the crooked floors. Some of the piers supporting the floors of the rental had collapsed. It was like living on a ship in rough seas. We had to prop books under china cabinets and book shelves to keep them from toppling over.

The night before we were going to get to see the inside of the Allen House for the first time and meet the owner in person, Rebecca and I and the kids stopped in front of the house and gazed at it. Almost right away, I noticed a woman sitting in the second-story window of the round south turret. Joshua, who was seven, said, "Who's that lady?"

"Must be the owner. Miss Marilyn," I said. (I was already picking up the Southern habit of putting "Mr." and "Miss" in front of people's first names.)

"Yeah, there she is," Rebecca said.

The woman in the window appeared to be sitting at a desk, reading a book or perhaps writing a letter by long hand.

Rebecca said, "Maybe we shouldn't sit here. She might get annoyed. She'll think we're stalking her or something."

When Rebecca and I returned the next evening, the porch didn't seem nearly as creepy to me without the radio evangelist shouting from the house about fire and brimstone. When Marilyn opened the door and ushered us in, I was pleased to see that the inside of the house looked much better than the outside. Chandeliers glittered softly overhead, the rooms were crowded with fancy antiques, and the walls were covered with gilt-framed prints and paintings.

As we walked through the first-floor rooms, Marilyn kept saying the house was "solid as a rock" and the most beautiful home she personally had ever been in, with the exception of the governor's mansion. "I can't believe I'm even thinking of selling my palace," she said, her voice whispery, her peppermint breath in my face, her capped teeth glistening behind her full crimson-colored lips. She batted her incredibly long eyelashes, and her bosom reminded me of the protrusions on the front bumper of a 1958 Cadillac. "It's gorgeous, gorgeous," she said.

I agreed.

"One of a kind," she said. "You'll never find another house like this. Oh, when I walk down the grand staircase, I feel like a queen."

The rooms glittered with crystal knickknacks and polished brass. Marilyn's fingers, as she gestured, glittered with diamonds and sapphires. She said that all the lumber used in the construction of the house came from Joe Lee Allen's personal timberlands and that nothing but four-hundred-year-old oak and heart of pine was used. The stained glass was made by glass blowers in New Orleans, the curved window frames in St. Louis. The ornate hand-beaten tin ceiling in the dining-room was crafted on site. There was no other ceiling like it in the *world*, she insisted. Cherub faces stared down at the dining room table.

In each room, pictures of Jesus and crucifixes hung on the walls. Even in the bathroom, a picture of a blue-eyed Jesus was perched above the faucets of the antique claw-foot tub.

Marilyn's bedroom was on the first floor. It was dominated by rich red fabrics, silver-framed mirrors, and more pictures of Jesus. "I know what you're thinking," she said. "Looks like a brothel. But I think it's gorgeous."

"Yes, it's lovely," Rebecca assured her.

Rebecca agreed with Marilyn that everything about the house, including her furniture and decorations, was fabulous.

Marilyn led us back to the foyer, and we followed her up the grand staircase (the servants' staircase was in the back of the house). On the second-floor landing, she spread her arms wide to emphasize the spaciousness of the hallway. "It's like a whole room!" Then she opened the door to the master bedroom, which included the south turret. We couldn't enter the room because it was packed full of boxes and furniture. Rebecca and I looked at each other and said simultaneously, "We saw you in the turret window last night."

"Oh, no, I haven't been in this room in months. I just use it for storage. I wasn't even here last night."

"Oh," I said. I had been thinking that she didn't look like the woman I had seen in the window, but I figured she just looked different from a distance.

Rebecca was more persistent than I was: "But we saw you ... or someone in the window last night."

"Well, as you can see, dear, it's not even possible to get to the window."

Rebecca and I nodded.

Then Marilyn put her hands on her narrow waist and arched her back. When she took an audible breath, it emphasized her physical attributes. "Have you heard the house is haunted?" The words slid past her crimson lips as a sigh.

After hesitating, I said, "Oh, yes," and nodded and grinned. I wanted to let her know we'd heard such foolishness but were unconcerned.

"Well, it is," she said. "It most definitely is. You need to know that. But it's nothing to worry about. As a matter of fact, it's the best security system you could ask for. All the thieves around here are scared to death of the place. They won't get near it. I intentionally let the outside look bad to enhance the impression that it's a haunted house. I say let the weeds grow, let the paint peel. The worse the place looks the more scared people are of it."

Rebecca and I both nodded. Rebecca said, "That's very clever."

"Nobody bothers me. The kids with their school fundraisers, the Girl Scouts, the salesmen—they keep right on going. But the ghosts are really nothing to worry about. When I first moved here they wouldn't leave me alone. I'd just be sitting in the parlor looking at a Dillard's catalog, and they'd start whispering. So I'd shout, 'In the name of Jesus Christ our Lord, leave me alone!'"

Rebecca gave me a look that let me know my mouth was open.

"I sprinkled holy water in every room and prayed. They're pretty quiet most of the time now," Marilyn continued. "If they start up, I just say, 'I'm not talking to you. The only spirit

I'm talking to in this house is the spirit of the Lord!'" She smiled at us radiantly. "So you'll have nothing to worry about."

Rebecca and I nodded. "That's good to know," I said.

DÉJÀ VU

At a professional convention in Little Rock in October 2005, one of my colleagues from the university introduced me to the man who took the famous photo of his wife in the Allen House dining room in the late 1960s, the photo in which a female ghost hovered beside his wife. My colleague had told this man that I was trying to buy the Allen House, and the man was eager to confirm all the paranormal stories. The photo, he said, was absolutely real. He also said he was present the day one of the other tenants refused to stay one more day because his furniture got moved around. "I still have dreams about that house," he said. "All these years later."

This man seemed perfectly normal, at least as normal as any of us in academia. We talked for a half hour or so and then had to attend separate meetings. The last thing he said to me was, "Good luck trying to buy it. And if you buy it, good luck."

ဆ ော

Amazingly, Rebecca and I settled on a price with Marilyn, a price that we thought was quite reasonable, and we gave her a deposit. When the appraisal came in, it was higher than the purchase price. She was a bit miffed and even said she hoped we didn't feel too bad about "robbing" her. She said we had caught her at just the right time, though, and she was ready to get out of Monticello because she was more a "Dallas kind of gal." Our buying the house must have been destined. "The Lord must have sent you," she said.

It would be two years, though, before we actually owned the house. Closing date after closing date would come, and Marilyn would cancel. In all, we scheduled a closing on about half a dozen different dates. The day before each of these closing dates, Marilyn called. Her voice crackling and breathy, she did not *request* more time but informed us that she absolutely *had to have* more time. She needed to hire a lot of help to get packed. She needed to auction off some things. She was having heart palpitations. And it was simply very emotionally traumatic for her to give up the house. She had even thought on several occasions about dismantling it and moving it with her to another state.

Although she was the one to cancel the closings, she insisted we give her more money to renew the contract on the purchase. We did. We really wanted the Allen House. We did, however, realize after a few months that it might be a long time before we actually got to live there and decided to look for another old and interesting house we could buy and live in while we waited. One day Rebecca was driving around and, by chance, turned down a little side street and saw a rundown, chocolate-brown Victorian that she found absolutely charming. She decided we could buy it and fix it up while we were waiting to get the Allen House, and we would at least be able to get away from the cramped rental house with its crooked floors. The chocolate-brown house didn't have a for-sale sign in front of it, but Rebecca was undaunted, as usual. Again, as she had in regard to the Allen House, she informed me that she would "make it happen"—and she did.

After we purchased the chocolate-brown Victorian, we discovered that it had first been the home of Sylvester Hotchkiss (1842–1909), a Chicago-trained architect and the only Union veteran of the Civil War buried in the town cemetery (he was placed off away from the Confederate veterans). Most interesting to us was the fact that he had designed the Allen House.

No one ever suggested to us that the Hotchkiss House was haunted, but people were eager to tell us that a man had hanged himself in the third-story stairwell after his lover ended their relationship. The twelve-year-old next-door neighbor, Buddy, reminded our small sons of the suicide on almost a daily basis, always adding something like, "Don't that disturb ya'll? Don't you lay awake at night just thinkin' 'bout it? That guy danglin' in your staircase by his neck. I hear he used a chain that cut good and deep into his windpipe. I'd have nightmares ever night if I had to sleep in your house. I'd pee the bed."

Tow-headed and ruddy-faced, Buddy seldom left his own yard, which was surrounded by a six-foot-high chain-link fence. He'd call to Jacob and Joshua to come over to the fence, and then he lectured them from the other side. Working nearby in the yard while he illuminated my sons about the quality of life in our community, I got the impression that Monticello had an incredible number of child molesters, serial killers, and alien abductions.

One day, he was telling us that Monticello had a real haunted house. "A real one. Not some fake one like at Halloween with mirrors and actors and fake blood," he said with great enthusiasm. It was called the Allen House, he told them. "I know a boy that snuck in there last year and went to the top floor, to the attic, and he never come down. *Never.* Don't nobody ever come down from that attic at the Allen House."

I said, "I've been in the Allen House. I've even been in the attic."

Buddy's eyes grew huge. "Dang! You're the only person ever come out alive!"

෴ ෴

It seemed most of Monticello knew we were in the process of buying the Allen House, and a lot of folks became very concerned about what we would do to the Allen House after we turned the Hotchkiss House into a "painted lady"— three shades of blue and two shades of gold. Some people were downright horrified. They seemed to believe that the only truly appropriate color for a historic home was white. Blue was okay, we were informed by several strangers, only for a porch ceiling. A blue porch ceiling was a tradition, we were told, because it kept flies and wasps away. It had something to do with the insects thinking the blue porch ceiling was the sky. The blue porch ceiling also kept away evil spirits because they couldn't cross a blue threshold. But it wasn't "right" to paint *most* of a house blue. People said, "Ya'll must be Yankees." We said we were from Oklahoma. "Yep, ya'll Yankees."

A woman who lived near the Allen House even came over to see us at the Hotchkiss House one Sunday afternoon to tell us she certainly hoped we weren't planning to paint the Allen House blue. "It's not really any of my business and you have the right to paint a house whatever color you want, but keep in mind what people will think. Ya'll plan to live in Monticello permanently?"

Some people thought the Hotchkiss House was beautiful painted up in blues and golds, a big improvement over the chocolate-brown, but Marilyn even told us the whole deal on her house was off—regardless of the Lord's intentions—if we were planning to paint it anything other than white. We had merely thought that the tall, narrow design of the Hotchkiss House with its three front porches and gingerbread lent itself to a painted-lady style. We assured Marilyn and everyone else that we felt that white was the only color for the Allen House.

⁂

The months passed. On three occasions I went to the Allen House to negotiate a renewal of the purchase contract. Rebecca was so frustrated with the delays she didn't accompany me to the negotiations out of fear that she would blurt out something that might offend Marilyn, causing her to call off the whole deal, disassemble the house, and move it to Dallas—instead of selling it to us.

Marilyn always looked as though she were ready for a night on the town, her hair and make-up perfect, her clothes expensive. She glittered under the chandeliers and always gave me a tour of the house as if I were seeing it for the first time. She sashayed slowly through the rooms, praising the house's beauty and uniqueness, and she repeated the story about how she'd performed a ritual to subdue the spirits.

She had learned a few things from her father, a carpenter, she said, and she gave me advice about making repairs and doing renovations. And she talked about living in the Middle East with a former husband, a husband she might still be married to if he had loved this house the way she did, the way Rebecca and I obviously did.

Marilyn told me that Rebecca and I and the kids were welcome to come over and work in the yard any time we wanted to, to think of the yard as our own, and we often did go over on the weekends with mowers and rakes and pruning shears. Working in the yard made us feel that we really were going to own the property some day.

∽๑ ๑∾

Finally, in June 2007, Rebecca and I became the fourth owners of Joe Lee Allen's 1906 gift to his beloved wife, Caddye, and their three daughters, Lonnie, Ladell, and Lewie.

Marilyn stayed on in the house for a couple of weeks because it was so hard for her to let go of the place. She finally left at midnight of the absolute last day she could remain, followed by the last of four moving vans. We learned from a neighbor that Marilyn had gone to a motel in Monticello and had stayed for two weeks, the moving vans in the motel parking lot, while she attempted to recover from the ordeal of giving up her palace.

∽๑ ๑∾

On moving day, as the kids and I were leaving the Hotchkiss House with a truck full of furniture, our neighbor Buddy called to us from behind his fence: "I feel sorry for ya'll! Ain't nobody ever gonna deliver a pizza to that haunted house, ya know!"

I had to reassure Bronte, Joshua, and Jacob that we would still be able to have pizzas delivered, even if we had to pay extra and meet the delivery man at the end of the driveway. The kids seemed relieved.

Also on moving day, a group of five teen-age boys came to the front door of the Allen House and said to Rebecca, "We wanta see inside your house. We hear it's haunted."

Rebecca explained that the house was our private residence and not open to the public. They sighed, threw up their arms, and peevishly stomped their feet. One of them said, "I been wanting to see this place all my life."

They were only the first indication of the public's interest in seeing the house and learning more about its ghosts. Marilyn had allowed no one in the house in years. On Halloween, she hired security guards to make sure no one set foot on her property.

The teenage boys were a reminder, in the midst of the excitement and labor of the move, that we were now the owners of a famous haunted house. But they weren't the only or most provocative reminder, by any means.

As I carried three heavy and cumbersome boxes up the side steps and through the side door, I glimpsed Jacob, who was five, standing quite still next to the servants' staircase, looking at me blankly, saying nothing. He looked pale, and I thought he might be sick. I turned away from him and set the stack of boxes down in front of the staircase, saying, "So how you like your new house?" Jacob said nothing. As I straightened the top box to assure it wouldn't topple, I said, "So you like it? Huh?" Still no answer. "You okay?" Then I turned ... and Jacob had vanished into thin air. The episode was odd, but I wiped the sweat from my eyes and went back to my job of carrying boxes into the house.

A few minutes later I found Jacob upstairs. He was watching his favorite *Star Wars* movie. "Hey, there you are," I said. "I wondered where you disappeared to."

"What?" He stared at a light-saber battle. Darth Vader was about to strike down Ben, Luke Skywalker's Jedi mentor.

"You were downstairs, and all of a sudden you disappeared."

"I wasn't downstairs. Not since Mom made lunch."

"But you were just downstairs. Like ten minutes ago."

"No." After a pause, he said, "You must be seein' things, Dad."

I let it go. But this was only the first in a series of similar incidents. A few days later, Rebecca came downstairs to breakfast and asked Jacob, who was already sitting at the table, how he got downstairs so fast. When I told her that he had been downstairs and sitting at the table with me for the past twenty minutes, she shook her head and said she had just seen him upstairs not half a minute before. I assured her that Jacob had been downstairs with me for at least twenty minutes.

She then told me that she had seen Jacob go into the downstairs bathroom the day before, never saw him come out, but then saw him upstairs a half hour later. She asked him why he had been in the downstairs bathroom so long. He said he hadn't been in the downstairs bathroom. He added that he didn't like to use that bathroom because it was "scary." In fact, I had noticed one day that although Jacob was playing downstairs he went all the way upstairs to use the bathroom and then came back down. I hadn't given it much thought at the time.

"And that's not all," Rebecca said. "Three days ago I guess it was, I was here in the kitchen and saw Jacob through the doorway turning the corner into the bathroom. Then a second later I saw him again, turning the corner into the bathroom."

I told her I didn't understand.

"It was like déjà vu. I saw him. Then I saw the exact same thing. Like a film clip looping twice. An instant replay." She said she kept looking through the kitchen doorway, expecting to see Jacob come out of the bathroom, but he never did. Finally, she went to the bathroom and the door was closed. She knocked. No answer. She opened it, and no one was in there.

We would soon get used to that first-floor bathroom door being closed most of the time. It seemed to close on its own. I even tested it one day to see whether it swung easily on its hinges. I theorized that maybe it closed whenever the air conditioning kicked on. I found that it did not close easily. Someone had to push or pull it shut. Rebecca said that our cat, which followed her all over the house when it was hungry, would never follow her into that bathroom. It would follow her into closets and other bathrooms—anywhere—but if she went into that bathroom, it would stop abruptly, back away and just wait for Rebecca to come out.

At the time, I was still in denial about there being ghosts in the house. In fact, I was still uncertain what I believed in regard to ghosts in general. We had lived in an old house in Oklahoma, and I would often awake in the middle of the night to voices. I was always certain the kids had left a TV on upstairs. Then I would go upstairs and find the TV off and cold to my touch. Rebecca thought we might have ghosts in that house. The people who were supposed to buy our Oklahoma house after leasing it for six months broke the contract and moved out, claiming the house was haunted. I was shocked that they couldn't come up with a better excuse for breaking the contract, and I was awestruck that they would suggest something so outrageous.

I tended to believe there had to be another explanation for what Rebecca and our children and I were experiencing in the Allen House. Besides, I didn't want people thinking I was nutty. I had a responsible and high-profile position at the university, and my boss, the Provost, was a very pragmatic and serious man whose respect I did not want to lose.

Jacob seemed oblivious to his ghostly double. But one day he did become furious with his older brother, Joshua, for trying to scare him by whispering his name over and over: *Jacob, Jacob, Jacob*. When Rebecca and I investigated Jacob's accusation, we discovered that Joshua had been in his own room, with his door shut, listening to music through earphones. We, however, allowed Jacob to continue thinking it was his big brother whispering his name.

∽ ∾

In those first days, my explorations focused on the dilapidated carriage house. One day, I pulled back a loose board on a wall and discovered a marble tombstone. It was just sitting there in a niche in the wall. Engraved with the inscription "Our Darling One Hath Gone Before to Greet Us on the Blissful Shore," it was for a boy born in 1895 and who died in 1900.

The Carriage House

On a window frame nearby, someone had written with a pencil "Ghost!"

The same day I discovered the tombstone, a family friend stopped by to visit. When Rebecca opened the door immediately after the friend had rung the doorbell, she expressed surprise and asked Rebecca how she got downstairs so quickly.

When Rebecca said she was already downstairs, the friend insisted that as she approached the house she had seen Rebecca (she was certain it was Rebecca) in an upstairs window.

The same friend had a joint yard sale with Rebecca at our house a couple of weeks later. In preparing for the sale, the friend was carrying items through the front door, past the parlor and library and setting them in the hallway. Rebecca, who was working in the back of the house, kept hearing her friend talking. Just the two of them were in the house. Eventually, she heard the friend calling, "Hey, Rebecca, where did you go?"

Rebecca hollered back, and her friend came to the back room and said, "You're a big help!"

"What do you mean?"

"I kept asking you to help me carry stuff and you just kept standing there in the library."

Rebecca explained that she had been in the back room the whole time. "I was wondering who you were talking to."

"You weren't in the library?" the friend asked.

"No, I just told you. I've been here tagging these things for the sale."

"Then who was in the library?"

Rebecca shrugged. "It wasn't me."

Her friend's eyes widened, her body stiffened. "Listen, you're going to come help me carry this stuff, and you're not leaving me alone in this house anymore."

◌ Chapter 4 ◌

THE PARTY PLACE

On the door frame inside the closet in the master bedroom, someone had written in pencil the name "Lonnie Lee," a five-digit phone number, and a Little Rock address.
Below that was the phrase "Lewie's telephone," another phone
number, and the year "1937" followed by "'47." Written twice
was the note "House built 1906." There were lists of numbers
and what appeared to be grocery lists. I was fascinated by the
thought that it could be Caddye or Ladell's handwriting. In a
couple of years, a discovery in the attic would confirm that the
writing on the door frame was Ladell's.

After we moved in, Rebecca's and my interest in the
house's history and in its original residents grew. The tombstone in the wall of the carriage house made me want to find
out anything I could about Houston Meredith, the boy who
died in 1900. It was odd that the tombstone pre-dated the house.
According to newspaper records, the carriage house was built
in 1907, the year after the main house was completed. So how
did the tombstone come to be in the wall? In doing library

and Internet research, I couldn't find any records of a Meredith family in Monticello, but there were some Merediths in northern Louisiana. The Allens had lots of employees, and the carriage house was built for servants, so I assumed that Houston Meredith had been the child of employees. But I had no answer to the question of why the tombstone predated the construction of the carriage house or why it was in the wall.

Although I had left the tombstone in its niche and was very hesitant to touch it because I found it incredibly creepy, I decided to inspect the tombstone more carefully. Something at the top of it had been broken off. I guessed that a Victorian cherub was probably missing. More significantly, the bottom of the marble tombstone was stained from being in the ground. It seemed clear the tombstone had been removed from a grave site, but where and when and why?

One possibility I considered was that the Meredith clan had moved to Monticello from Louisiana sometime after 1907 and brought the tombstone with them. If so, the big questions were: Did they also bring the boy's body? And if they did, where was the body buried?

I kept in mind that the Allens lived on the property for about fifteen years before they built the mansion. They first lived in a small house that was built in the 1880s. That original Allen House had been moved across the street. The Allens had servants throughout the 1890s. Perhaps the Merediths lived on the property at that time rather than later. Perhaps Houston Meredith was buried on the spot where Joe Lee Allen later decided he wanted a big eight-room carriage house.

I spent a good bit of time digging up old bricks out of the yard to use in making walkways. I had found several places in the yard where bricks from nineteenth-century buildings were dumped in a hole and covered up. Whenever I started digging, especially around the carriage house, Rebecca would say she worried about what I might dig up besides bricks.

Early in our research, we wondered about the sightings of the ghosts of children. The Allen daughters all lived to be middle-aged. The Allens' one son died at nine months. We couldn't help wondering whether five-year-old Houston Meredith might be wandering about. We also read that the first building on the land was the Rodgers Female Academy, founded in 1857. During the Civil War, classes were suspended, and the building was used as a hospital for Confederate soldiers wounded in local battles. After the Civil War, the school was reopened as the Wood Thompson School for Boys. Later, it became coeducational. And in the first decade of the twentieth century, according to newspaper notices, school for third, fourth, and fifth grades was offered in "The Allen Brick on North Main Street."

The year we moved in, our daughter, Brontë, was eleven. She was more interested in the history of the house than either Joshua or Jacob and often asked me questions about the original owners. She also seemed sensitive to the presence of spirits. From the first day in the Allen House, she said she felt she was being watched by "some boy." The television in her room would turn itself on at all hours of the day, and sometimes it would wake her in the middle of the night.

One morning after I had gone to work, Rebecca and the boys left Brontë, who was still sleeping, at the house alone while they ran errands. When they returned, Brontë was in the yard, walking nervously in circles. She was very relieved they were back. She had woken up and found everyone gone, but she didn't exactly feel alone. In fact, she was certain she was not alone—so she had run outside.

∽◎ ◎∾

I loved exploring the huge attic—as long as it was during the day or as long as someone was with me at night. During a bad rain storm one night, Rebecca asked me whether I was going to go up to the attic to check the buckets we kept under roof leaks. The idea of going up there alone during the storm really didn't appeal to me. I insisted to her that everything up there was fine. I was sure. Then our bedroom ceiling started to leak. A large puddle formed at the foot of our bed, and Rebecca was not happy. So I had to go up there.

The attic stairs creaked. Lightning flashed. Thunder crashed. Rain pounded the metal roof, and water dripped from the rafters. I emptied the buckets as quickly as I could. I put them back in their spots and hustled downstairs. Not that I expected a ghost to jump out at me, but it was awfully creepy. Lending to its character and creepiness was the fact that nearly the entire attic ceiling and all the rafters were charred black from a 1909 fire.

Nonetheless, I enjoyed treasure hunting … investigating dark corners and looking under floorboards up there. Among my first discoveries were three cast-iron World War I "doughboy" toy soldiers; letters, cards, and school papers from the 1920s and 1930s bearing the name "Allen Bonner"; part of a horse bridle; a child's shoe; an early twentieth-century doll's hand; a cardboard "paper doll" that had been

The Attic

packaged in a coffee can around 1895, the way baseball cards in that era were packaged with chewing tobacco; Sunday School certificates dated from 1917 to 1923 that belonged to Mamie McKennon, who I soon learned was Caddye's old-maid sister; a hand-drawn map of Monticello signed by "Carl Leidinger" with the Allen House prominently marked by a circle of stars and, mysteriously, the words "Mr. Bruiser."

In another corner, I found half of a photograph of an infant. Enough of the inscription on the back was intact to determine that it said "Miss Ladell." It was eerie and fascinating to find this item associated with a woman I had read about in a dozen articles on the house's paranormal history. *Why would someone rip a photo of a baby in half?* I wondered. *And why that of Ladell, a woman who at age fifty-four decided life was not worth living?* No one knew why Ladell had killed herself. There seemed to even be confusion about how she died.

Some articles and books said she took potassium cyanide. Other sources said it was mercury cyanide. Rebecca and I had had townspeople insist to us that she hanged herself. In any case, she had wanted to die, and as I held that partial photo from 1894 in my hand, I vividly imagined Ladell herself tearing that old picture and flinging the pieces toward the dark corner of the attic. What disappointment or frustration had befallen a woman whose rich daddy had named a town after her? I had already learned that the town of Ladelle, Arkansas, was named for her in 1912. Joe Lee, the chief investor in the town, didn't name it after his oldest daughter, Lonnie Lee, or his youngest, Lewie, or even for his deceased infant son, Walter, but for his middle daughter. What made her the special one? Newspaper social notes from the early twentieth century indicated a life of travel, private schools, and parties for all the Allen daughters.

Speaking of parties, in a history of the local Presbyterian Church, I read that the Allens were always associated with parties. Joe Lee and Caddye hosted many celebrations in their home and at the hotel they owned, the Allen Hotel, which had forty guest rooms and an amazing number of bathrooms for the early twentieth century: eight. One for every five guest rooms!

In the 1930s, the attic of the Allen House was known as "the party place of Monticello." The church history said that Karl (sometimes spelled "Carl") Leidinger, Jr., the son of the oldest Allen daughter, Lonnie Lee, was a popular boy growing up in the Allen House with his parents and his grandmother and that he frequently had friends over.

Although the church history said not one word about Ladell or *her* son, Allen Bonner also lived in the house during the 1920s and 1930s. The ghost stories said he haunted the attic because it had been his special play area and, later, his study room.

In the third-story turret room one day, I dusted off a small home-made desk built against the wall and discovered that Allen Bonner had written on it with white paint: "Ye Olde Village Half Wits," it said. And there were three names: "Keats Henry," "Jeanne Lipscomb," and "Allen Bonner." And there was a date: January 20, 1932. There were planks laid across the rafters of the turret that I had not given much thought to, but when I looked up from the desk, I noticed an opening in those planks and theorized that the desk also served as a ladder, a sort of step stool, to allow a kid to gain access to the turret. He could pull himself up through the opening and sit inside there on the planks, hidden in his own clubhouse. When I removed the planks, I found evidence to support my theory: remnants of a toy airplane, old radio parts, a *Chicago Tribune* newspaper from the 1930s, an old-fashioned photographic plate on which the image had faded away completely, and a large, wicked-looking homemade paddle that grandmother probably used for disciplining children … until one day it disappeared.

The south turret room in the attic was furnished with a very old couch and overstuffed chair. It was easy to imagine Allen Bonner and Karl Leidinger, Jr., and their friends lounging about. Allen Bonner was probably the life of the party. I eventually discovered his nickname was "Duke" and that he

Writing on the Desk

wrote a humorous column in 1934 called "The Lowdown" for the Arkansas A & M newspaper, *The Southeasterner*:

> While I was in the store the other day some one came in and informed everybody it was raining cats and dogs outside. Doubting their word I stepped outside and darned if they weren't right,—I stepped right in a poodle!

When he transferred to Baylor University his junior year, Allen Bonner wrote for the Baylor newspaper *The Daily Lariat* and joined the notorious Nose Brotherhood, a campus organization of jokers and pranksters.

Some of the old school papers I found in the attic were Allen Bonner's written efforts at jokes and humorous skits.

The South Turret

Under a floorboard, I found a small British publication entitled "Art Catalogue for 1934." I immediately and simply assumed that Allen Bonner had been a young man with an interest in art. Then I opened the catalogue to find that it was full of photos of naked women.

∽◦ ◦∾

Rebecca and I spent most of our spare time fixing up the house. We had a carpenter do some repairs on the collapsed porch roof, but otherwise we did things ourselves—mainly because we worked cheaper than anyone else.

When the weather was good, I painted the exterior. At night and in bad weather, I painted the interior. Rebecca was becoming an expert at wallpapering.

Although the interior of the house had looked good when it was crammed full of Marilyn's fancy things, it looked bad when it was empty. All the walls needed wallpapering or painting. And because Marilyn took most of the light fixtures, electrical wires dangled from the ceilings.

Rebecca's sister and brother-in-law came to visit just a couple of weeks after we moved in, and the first thing Rebecca's brother-in-law said upon entering the house was, "So how long was this place abandoned?"

One Saturday I was precariously hanging out an attic window, painting the north third-story gable and risking my life in the name of architectural preservation. After I had been at the job most of the afternoon, I pulled myself inside and enjoyed the bliss of sure footing.

I looked across the attic and noticed an interesting play of light and shadow in the south turret room. It intrigued me that somehow my shadow—my torso and shoulders and head—was cast all the way across the attic and was present on the wall in that room. I even broke the silence of the attic by saying aloud to myself: "That's interesting." I also noticed the movement of a curtain on one of the turret windows.

Then I moved, watching my shadow. I moved again. But when I moved, my shadow did not.

I decided I had done enough painting that day and quickly went downstairs.

⊸ *Chapter 5* ⊷

TRICK OR TREAT

On the night we closed on the purchase of the house in June 2007, Marilyn had said to me, "Now remember, Mark, you'll have to hire security on Halloween to keep people away."

I thought for a moment and then joked, "I think I'll sell tickets instead." By October of that year, Rebecca and I were actually considering it.

The five teenage boys who had arrived the day we moved in and wanted to see our ghosts were just the beginning. During our first weeks in the house, other teenagers showed up at the door, usually two or three at a time, wide-eyed, stuttering, fidgeting, sweaty: "We … we were … were wonderin' if … if you'd … you'd let us see … see your house."

I always gaped, said, "Huh?"

"It would be … be so cool."

"Why?"

"Cause you got ghosts."

"I'm sorry. We're kind of busy right now, and besides, this is our home. We don't give tours. It's not a business."

"Oh. Well ... well ... you think you ever will?"

"Will what?"

"Give tours."

"No."

But eventually, Rebecca persuaded me to consider it. Her most persuasive argument connected to the fact that the renovation was costing a fortune, even though she and I were doing most of the repairs and improvements ourselves. I was working forty to fifty hours a week at the university and then working on the house every evening and all day Saturdays and Sundays and holidays. "It might be fun to give tours," Rebecca said. "We might make some money."

I shrugged. "Well, who knows? A few people might pay to see the house. Even if fifty show up we might make a few bucks."

It wasn't always teenagers who came to the front door wanting to see the house. One afternoon, three elderly ladies rang the doorbell. When I answered the door, a prune-faced woman with a hump on her back and wispy white hair like a wad of cobwebs, looked up at me and said, "Ladell home?"

"What?"

Another of the ladies bumped her aside and said, "What she means, sir ... what she intended to say ... was, is the house still haunted?"

I smiled, shaking my head. "No," I said. Then I shrugged. "Who knows about these things?"

"Have you seen anything?"

"Oh, you'd need to ask my wife about that."

The third lady, the youngest, who looked about seventy-five, said, "The people that used to live here said it was haunted, said they saw that woman that killed herself upstairs. They were the people that owned it after it was apartments. They fixed it up and had parties. People say they had psychics in and they did one of those ... one of those ... what you call ...?"

The one with the hump on her back hissed, "Séance."

"That's it. A séance. They let people come in and see the house. Just any time. They were so nice. I saw it in 1987. We thought you'd do the same."

"I'm sorry," I said. "We're just not set up for doing anything like that."

"We just want to look around."

"I'm really sorry, ladies."

"It's not right, young man, for you to keep a house like this all to yourself."

I thought, *My god, they're worse than the teenagers.*

"Come on, young man."

"Listen, we have small children!" I blurted. I wasn't sure what my point was, but finally the ladies left.

∽ ❧

In addition to strangers showing up at the door, paranormal investigators started calling and e-mailing the first week we were in the house, asking whether we would allow them in to capture evidence of the activity or to debunk it. Having paranormal investigators in our home was something we were going to have to spend some time thinking about, we told them.

We often noticed people standing in front of the house at all hours of the night and day taking photos. One person e-mailed us a night-time photo that showed the house with a kind of halo emanating from the widow's walk. The person claimed that the picture was not "Photoshopped."

One photo that Rebecca had taken of the exterior seemed to reveal several faces in the windows. One face was in the second-story south turret window and looked like the woman we had seen there the night before we saw the inside of the house for the first time. Rebecca and a lot of other people saw children's faces in the photo, looking out of the windows of the enclosed second-floor porch, and even a couple of dogs and a cat.

Always the skeptic, I laughed and pointed out that one of the images looked like Slimmer from the movie *Ghost Busters*. Just reflections, lights, and shadows, I said. But when faced with possible evidence of paranormal activity, I sometimes recalled a woman I shared an office with early in my teaching career in the mid-1980s. She was in her late fifties and a former nun. She told me she had lived for several years in a haunted convent. Everyone in the convent accepted it as haunted, and nearly everyone who stayed there for more than a few weeks saw the ghost of a nineteenth-century nun. Long-time residents were never surprised or scared when the deceased sister manifested, my office mate said. I remembered being amazed that someone so well educated and intelligent could be so convinced of the existence of ghosts.

I also sometimes thought of the widow of a friend who died suddenly of a heart attack at the age of forty-six. One day he seemed fine. The next day he was dead. This friend's widow told me that, for the first couple of weeks after his death, either her doorbell or her telephone would ring in the middle of the night at the exact time he had died. She always woke up and would look at the clock next to her bed. She would pick up the phone, but there would only be a dial tone. She would hurry to the front door, but no one was there.

⤳ ⤵

One night at about ten thirty, a school bus pulled up in front of our house. Its door folded back, and a swarm of high-school kids burst forth and raced through the front gate, up the walk and onto the porch. They slapped their palms against the side of the house and, screaming hysterically, raced back to the bus, which slammed its door and sped off like a muscle car.

Finally, Rebecca and I decided we really would sell tickets on Halloween. We hired and trained three college students to give dignified, informative, educational historical tours. I insisted that we would do nothing corny. Because I was still uncertain about ghosts in general and Allen House ghosts in particular and because I feared the ridicule of people I respected, our tours would emphasize the history we'd learned about the Allen family and the architecture of the house.

A Little Rock television station learned we were giving tours of our famous haunted house and sent a camera crew a couple of days before Halloween. A reporter interviewed Rebecca, mainly pressing her on the question of whether she'd seen any ghosts, to which Rebecca finally relented and talked about the weird sightings of our son Jacob in places where he claimed not to be. The narration of the story when it aired emphasized the house's reputation over the decades for paranormal activity. The cameraman got lots of footage of peeling paint and rotting wood and shredded wallpaper. The segment ran for three or four minutes on the evening news and again on the late news.

Halloween came, and over 600 people showed up. They were lined up down the sidewalk and around the corner. We hadn't hired enough college students, so Rebecca and I started giving tours ourselves. Our guests nodded as our tour guides told of the important role Joe Lee Allen had played in the economic development of our small community and of how the architecture reflected the blending of neoclassical, Queen Anne, and Gothic styles. And the guests nodded as our guides pointed to the curved glass and the stained glass, to the fancy moldings in the front rooms where the family spent their time and the plain moldings in the back of the house where the servants spent theirs. They also nodded and squinted at the cherub faces in the tin ceiling of the dining room, but inevitably, people would grow impatient and say, "Yeah, yeah, yeah. That's nice about the neo-whatever, but let's hear about the ghosts."

In the months and years to come I found that when people came to the house or when I was invited to talk about the Allen family history to clubs, civic groups, or historical societies, what people mostly wanted to hear was the ghost stories—even if they initially claimed they had no interest in such "foolishness." I could spend an hour or two discussing history, economics, politics, and architecture, and when I asked whether there were any questions, somebody would raise their hand swiftly and say, "Tell us about the ghosts." One time I visited a high school in another town to talk about literature, and in the middle of my discussion of William Faulkner, Flannery O'Connor, and Kate Chopin, a student raised her hand and asked, "Dean Spencer, don't you own the Allen House?" When I said yes, the high-school kids were finished hearing about literature. They wanted to talk about ghosts. Their teachers did, too.

ભ૦ ૭ભ

Our tour guests seemed to enjoy getting to see the house. That first Halloween it was still rather dilapidated, so it possessed the look of a "haunted house." Some people would suddenly shiver as they walked through a room. A lot of them shivered as they stood in the master bedroom and heard about Ladell's suicide. "She killed herself *here?*" The person would point at the floor. "In this room?" They got wide-eyed when the lights unexplainably flickered. We really weren't manipulating the lights, but when we were in the master bedroom and we started talking about Ladell, the lights would flicker.

"Why did she kill herself?" many people asked.

"Nobody knows," I said to my own tour groups. "She was divorced. Her son had died. It was the holiday season. A lot of people get depressed around the holidays, you know. We just don't know." I shrugged. I, of course, had no notion that in less than two years I would discover one Saturday morning the answer to that question people had been asking since 1948: "Why did Ladell do it?"

Along with the artifacts we had found on the property and displayed during the tour—the toy soldiers, the doll parts, the wine and rum bottles, the school papers, the half-photo of infant Ladell—we displayed a postcard of the house we had found on eBay. It was from about 1908, giving us a wonderful image of how the house appeared when it was

The Master Bedroom

first built. There had been railings on the porch roofs that were no longer present, and the second-story porch was not enclosed. An anomaly that I noticed in the post-card photo but that I had never mentioned to anyone, not even to Rebecca, was on the left side of the house's front steps. It was probably just a trick of light and shadows, I told myself, but I would often stare at that spot on the picture. It looked to me like a ghostly image of a little boy standing on the steps. Then during the Halloween tour, a teenage boy said to me, "Hey, did you ever notice the ghost in that old postcard?"

"What do you mean?" I said.

The teenager pointed to the ghost boy that I always saw and said, "Right there. There's some kid standing on the steps."

A lady who looked as though she was in her sixties said to me at the end of the tour, "I think I saw Ladell upstairs. I saw a woman in an old-fashioned dress come out of the master bedroom, cross the hall, and go into your children's toy room. There were other people in the hall, but I don't think anybody else saw her."

I just said, "Wow. Thanks for letting me know."

෴ ෴

A lot of people thanked Rebecca and me profusely for allowing them to come inside our house. They said they loved seeing it. They complimented us on the way we were fixing it up. They were glad we were painting the exterior white and not blue.

Some people were shocked to learn that we actually lived in the house. "How can you stand it? Aren't you scared?"

I was reminded of the neighbor boy, Buddy, over at the Hotchkiss House. I had not seen him among the tour guests. I supposed he was too frightened and didn't want to take the chance of being lured to that attic.

"No. We're not scared," Rebecca and I answered.

All seemed good after our Halloween tours. All had gone well. Nothing got broken. No one fell down the stairs. And we had made some money to use on renovations.

In the days and weeks in the fall of 2007, we found ourselves fielding even more requests from late-night-radio talk-show hosts and paranormal investigators. We gave tours by appointment to Cub Scout troops, ladies book clubs, and cheerleader squads. People wanted to get married at the house. In fact, two couples who had their first date at our Halloween tour ended up getting married at the Allen House.

One annoyance at the time, though, was that Rebecca had started to misplace things on a daily basis. She was always frantically searching for her keys or her purse or her watch or a brush or a pen. "I would have sworn I put it on my dresser," she'd say, but she would find it in the master bathroom. "I could swear I put it on the kitchen table," but she would find it on a table in the upstairs hallway.

I would kid her that she was becoming senile at the age of thirty-two.

She said, "I think it's Allen Bonner."

⨭ Chapter 6 ⨮

SECRETS

Beneath the main house and the carriage house both, I found many old wine, rum, and bourbon bottles. Did someone sit under the house drinking? Not likely. The low crawl space would have been cramped and dark and dirty for anyone wanting to swill liquor in private. More likely, someone flung the bottles under the house to hide them, someone who didn't want them discovered in a trash pile or noticed by the town's garbage collectors.

In a dark and very dirty corner of the attic, tucked under an eave as though stuffed there like a secret, I picked up what I first thought was just a rag. But when I spread it open, I realized it was a girl's swimsuit from the first decade of the twentieth century. It was brown and white, had a V-neck and limp little bows on the shoulders. It had been scorched by the fire that nearly consumed the third floor in 1909. As when I found the partial 1894 photo of an infant, I had a vivid image of a middle-aged Ladell, this time balling up that swimsuit she had worn as the happy young daughter of a rich and doting father and flinging it into a far corner, miserable that she had lost her youth and her daddy and … and what else? Her husband? Her son?

∽◉ ◉◡

Joe Lee Allen died in 1917. One of his business ventures at that time was selling automobiles: Buicks and Dorts. According to his newspaper obituary, he had driven to Collins, Arkansas, in the early afternoon of October 23, a Tuesday, to demonstrate an automobile to a prospective customer on Main Street in the little town about sixteen miles from Monticello. While making his sales pitch, at about two o'clock, he suddenly collapsed, and some men quickly carried him into the nearby drug store, where the pharmacist frantically attempted to revive him. The pharmacist, however, soon declared him dead.

Joe Lee had had a heart attack earlier that year and had spent part of the summer recuperating in Michigan, where it was cooler. The newspaper announced his return to Monticello in late summer, saying his health was much improved. Joe Lee was president of one of the banks, and when word reached Monticello by telephone that he was dead, his banker friends loaded into their cars and drove to Collins to retrieve his remains. They brought him back to his house, where the funeral was held two days later, the body on display in the dining room beneath the four cherubs.

For some reason, I have always imagined that Ladell was the most devastated of the three Allen girls, and she must have hated being so far away—she was living with her husband, Boyd Bonner, in Greensburg, Indiana, at the time. Lewie, the youngest, was at school in Nashville. Lonnie Lee was living in Little Rock with her husband, Karl.

The Dining Room Ceiling

Caddye, who would for the rest of her life continue to refer to herself as "Mrs. Joe Lee Allen," had lost her husband of twenty-seven years. She and Joe Lee shared the experience of having lost their fathers when they were small children; they both loved parties; they both loved the Presbyterian Church; and they both loved money. The Allens had their own horse-drawn hearse, which they rented out for funerals, so maybe Caddye took a little comfort in saving money on Joe Lee's funeral. When Lonnie Lee and Karl came to live with her soon afterward, she charged them rent of ten dollars a month. She took in boarders starting in the 1920s. She certainly seemed concerned about money although, according to the local Presbyterian Church history, she doubled the family fortune after Joe Lee's death, mainly from her ownership of a movie theatre that Karl managed for her.

I imagine Caddye strong and pragmatic, Lonnie much like her mother, Lewie fragile but ultimately resilient. I have a feeling Ladell never quite got over her father's death, which occurred when she was twenty-three. She would choose to die at the same age her father did: fifty-four.

∽๑ ๑๑

In the university's archives, I found Ladell's obituary on the front page of the town's newspaper for January 6, 1949:

FUNERAL SERVICES HELD TUESDAY FOR MRS. LADELL BONNER

Funeral services for Mrs. Ladell Bonner, aged 54, were held in the family residence Tuesday morning at 10 o'clock conducted by the Rev. I. H. Williams, pastor of First Presbyterian Church of which she was a member. Interment followed in Oakland cemetery.

Born in Monticello March 22, 1894, the daughter of Mrs. J. L. Allen and the late Mr. Allen, she lived her entire life here where she was beloved by a wide circle of friends. She was prominently identified in civic and social life of Monticello.

Her only son, the late Allen Bonner, former Gazette Newsman and later with Associated Press in New York City, died in 1944.

Survivors include other than her mother one sister, Mrs. Karl Leidinger of Little Rock; three nephews, Dr. Karl Leidinger of Springfield, Mo., Robert Hale Jones, Jr., Lewis Allen Jones of Memphis, and a niece, Miss Martha Anne Jones of Memphis.

⁓ ⁓

Ladell's body, like her father's, had lain in the dining room beneath the cherub faces. I thought the absence of any mention of her divorce or of her cause of death was a reflection of the journalistic courtesies of the day and of the family's social prominence. Ladell's sister Lewie was, rightly, not listed as a survivor because she had died in September 1944 at the age of forty-six. Like their father, Lewie apparently suffered from a heart condition. Robert, Lewis, and Martha Anne Jones were Lewie's children.

The statement that Ladell had lived in Monticello all her life seemed a little odd because it simply was not true. Rebecca and I had already discovered through our research that Ladell had lived for a time in Dumas, Arkansas, and Greensburg, Indiana, her husband's hometown. According to the 1920 census, she and Boyd Bonner and their son were living in Ft. Worth, Texas. After her divorce in 1927 from Boyd, Ladell lived in Memphis where she managed a hotel, probably having gained such experience when she was younger at the Allen Hotel. Ladell had a roommate in Memphis named Clide, a widow in her thirties, the census stated. Interestingly, in the same building, another pair of roommates were also named Ladell and Clide, but the census indicated they were men. Allen Bonner lived in Monticello with his grandmother during that time.

On page 3 of the January 6, 1949, newspaper was a brief and unsigned eulogy:

> *The death of Mrs. Ladell Bonner, known fondly by her friends as Dell, has brought sadness to a wide circle of friends extending into many states. Possessed of a charming personality and lovable disposition, she believed that to be loved was to love others. She practiced her philosophy of life in her everyday living: never feeling that anything was too hard to do for a friend. A constant companion of her mother her first thought was always of her.*
>
> *She will be sadly missed in social and civic circles of Monticello.*

Rebecca and I gained some solid historical facts when we obtained an official copy of Ladell's death certificate from the state. It confirmed that her death was by suicide. Specifically, suicide by mercury cyanide poisoning. We had learned she died on January 2, 1949, when we found her grave in the Allen family plot in the local cemetery, along with Joe Lee's, Caddye's, baby Walter's, Lonnie Lee's, and Allen Bonner's. The death certificate showed that she had been admitted to the hospital on December 26. In addition to suggesting a long and gruesome death—an absolutely horrible ordeal— it shed new light on the story people persistently told about the suicide. Caddye was giving a party. Ladell had fixed herself a plate of hors d'ouvres, which she took along with a glass of punch to the master bedroom. Then she killed herself. Because of the date of death on her tombstone, we had assumed that the party was a celebration of New Year's. Now we realized it was a Christmas party.

As we exhausted library, historical archive, and Internet sources, Rebecca and I sought out residents of Monticello who might have memories of the Allens, or to whom stories of the Allens had been passed down.

A ninety-year-old man said he remembered that Caddye Allen made the best lemon pie he'd ever had. He had no recollection of Ladell or the other Allen girls. He knew nothing about Karl Leidinger, Jr., or Allen Bonner. This man had delivered groceries to the back door of the Allen House in the 1930s. He couldn't say whether Caddye was friendly or snobby or meek or loud or anything else, except that she gave him a wedge of lemon pie when he delivered the groceries.

An elderly woman remembered attending a birthday party (she couldn't remember whose) at the house and that she got to eat green shaved-ice. She remembered nothing except for that green shaved-ice, until she noticed our antique Victrola and said, "Oh! I remember the Victrola! I remember the music!" When I told her it belonged to Rebecca and me, and was not the Allens', she said, "Are you sure? They had one just like it."

Another woman told me that in the 1940s, when she was about nine years old, she and her mother visited Caddye Allen in her opulent bedroom after Caddye broke her hip. She thought Ladell was present, but she wasn't sure. In a hushed tone, she told me the "Allen secret," which was really no secret in those times, because everyone spoke of it: Ladell was addicted to liquor.

A lady in her nineties said she hadn't known Ladell but had heard about her. When I asked what she had heard about Ladell, this lady grinned slyly and, although we were alone, whispered, "She was *fast*."

I spoke on the phone with the eighty-nine-year-old son of the pharmacist who sold Ladell the mercury cyanide. He said his father felt profound guilt for selling Ladell the poison. His father often commented that the first week of 1949 was the worst he could remember because it was the week a deadly tornado struck the nearby town of Warren and was the week Ladell Allen Bonner died. He also told me that within weeks of Ladell's suicide, a woman who lived just around the corner from the Allen House had killed her-

Ladelle

self in the same manner as Ladell, with mercury cyanide, apparently to escape from a miserable marriage.

Rebecca and I drove to Ladelle, Arkansas, one Sunday afternoon and discovered, perhaps appropriately, Ladelle was largely a ghost town. Only ruins of the general store, post office, train depot, and jail remained. The crumbling main street of the town petered out into a field of weeds.

∽ ↷

"What's it like to live in the Allen House?" people always asked us. They wanted to know what we'd seen, what we'd heard, what we'd smelled, and what we'd felt.

I took pleasure in explaining away certain events and found natural explanations for many sounds and sights immediately after their occurrences: the wind, a draft, squirrels on the roof, birds on the roof, a cat jumping down from a table, the play of light and shadow, the normal moans and groans of a big old house. I really didn't want to admit what I was starting to suspect: maybe there was something to these ghost stories.

Our first Easter in the house, Rebecca walked into the front parlor and found the turntable of our antique Victrola spinning. No one had touched the Victrola in at least a month. As she stared at it, it spun faster and faster when it should have spun slower and slower. When she put the needle down to play the spinning record, it stopped instantly.

When Rebecca came upstairs to tell me about the Victrola, she glimpsed a man standing in the hallway—just for a second and then he was gone. He was wearing a large hat. She walked into the bedroom and said, "There was a man in the hall just now."

"A man?" I said. I was sitting on our antique love seat and had been reading. I looked up and saw that Rebecca was wearing her black T-shirt with the names of the witches executed in Salem in 1692 and that her face was pale and her eyes seemed strange.

She nodded. "A man wearing a big hat."

"Oh?" I said, my spine tingling. "Ah, who do you ... think the man is ... ah, was?"

She didn't say anything for a few seconds.

"Honey?" I said.

Then she seemed to snap out of her trance. "I don't know who he is. He had on that hat ... kind of like a cowboy hat, but he was flat like a shadow. He didn't have a face. Well—no facial features. No eyes or nose or mouth."

A few weeks later, Rebecca saw the man again, when she looked down the main staircase from the second-floor hallway. She just saw the back of him, but recognized the hat. He walked in the foyer toward the front door. When he got to the front door, he was suddenly gone.

The Foyer

∽ Chapter 7 ∾

THE SCENT OF LILACS
REDUX

The Monticello High School class of 1955 knew how to party. And not just in 1955. In the spring of 2008, the chair of the reunion committee for the class of '55 asked Rebecca and me whether they could have their reunion party at our house, in part because they would be honoring their best-known classmate, Carolyn Wilson, the author of the 1966 novel *The Scent of Lilacs,* which everybody knew was inspired by the Allen House. Carolyn had moved to Fayetteville, Arkansas, in the 1960s and became a highly successful real-estate broker and had not written another novel until 2007. At the reunion, Carolyn would have a book signing for her new novel and for a reprint edition of *The Scent of Lilacs.*

The members of the class of '55 had considered having the reunion at the Trotter House, a bed-and-breakfast down the street from us. The Trotter House was owned by the university, however, so alcoholic beverages were not allowed. The graduates of 1955 wanted their wine coolers.

Rebecca and I were thrilled at the prospect of meeting Carolyn Wilson and were happy to host her book signing and class-reunion party. The reunion committee advertised the event as open to the public so Carolyn could sell lots of books.

Out of curiosity, Rebecca and I had read *The Scent of Lilacs*—the story of a young bride who is harassed by what was possibly a ghost in her husband's old family mansion. It was clearly set in a house somewhat like the Allen House. The descriptions of the carriage house in the novel were particularly close to the lay-out and appearance of our carriage house. We had heard from a number of townspeople that when Carolyn lived in the house, she sensed a presence that was jealous of her or envied her as a new bride.

Carolyn's new novel was about a small town modeled on 1950s Monticello and focused on sexual scandals. The sex was pretty explicit. It was a kind of small-town *Valley of the Dolls* or *The Love Machine*. It was rather different from the innocent Gothic romance inspired by the Allen House. Her classmates and lots of other folks snatched up both the new book and *The Scent of Lilacs*. Our house was packed with boisterous partygoers who quickly consumed their wine coolers.

Carolyn's husband and one of their sons accompanied her to the party. She had serious respiratory problems and kept a breathing machine nearby. Her son and husband made sure she didn't wear herself out. Everyone knew she had only a few months to live, and it was nice for all of us to see the thrill in her eyes as she was showered with attention, fans congratulating her on the new book and the new edition of *Lilacs* and telling her how much they loved her writing.

His eyes shining with tears that he tried to hold back, her husband told me he had not seen Carolyn so happy in years.

Some of the people who showed up had driven from Louisiana, Texas, and Mississippi. One of the guests, a long-time business associate of Carolyn's, had driven down from northern Arkansas. She said to Rebecca, Carolyn's husband, and me, "So this is the famous haunted house."

Carolyn's husband said, "Damn right it is."

He and Carolyn had lived in the first-floor north-side rooms as newlyweds in 1959. He wandered into my study as Rebecca and I followed. "Our bed was right under these curved windows." He gazed nostalgically at the floor where their bed had apparently been, shaking his head.

Rebecca asked, "Did anything paranormal ever happen in here?"

He looked at her and gave her a little smile. "Nothing paranormal, honey, but some *supernatural* things definitely went on in here, if you know what I mean." He nodded. "Yeah. Supernatural. We were newlyweds, you know."

He didn't seem to remember much else, and Carolyn gave me a long stare when I asked her what she remembered about the house. Finally, she said, "For goodness sake, that was fifty years ago. You see if you remember anything after fifty years. I remember it made me want to write a book. That's about all."

Some of the guests, though, did share with us memories of the house. Some of them had walked past the house almost daily on their way to elementary school in the 1940s, but they couldn't recall seeing Ladell. They did, though, remember their parents talking about the suicide. Everybody wondered why she did it. Some of our guests had lived in the house in the 1960s or 1970s, when they were college students. They confirmed the stories about things getting moved around and sounds in the attic and the creepiness of the master-bedroom suite being locked up. One little woman who reminded me of the troll dolls that have a swath of brightly colored hair sticking straight up out of their heads gazed off back into her past and said she and her friends had "dropped a lot of acid" and "smoked a lot of weed in this house." I thought, *That might have explained a lot of the paranormal experiences.*

The mayor came. A state senator. The president of Commercial Bank, for whom Joe Lee Allen was a legendary figure in the world of local finance.

The party rocked on. The class of '55 was a good humored, bawdy, and loud bunch. They were determined to have a good time, and Rebecca and I were glad to be hosting them. They flashed lots of photos. Several people, though, complained that their camera batteries drained awfully fast.

In contrast to most of the revelers, one man I talked with was soft-spoken and philosophical. His white hair starkly contrasted with his black suit. He was gaunt, and his liver-spotted hands were bony, his fingers long. *He could have played an undertaker in the movies, or the grim reaper,* I thought. He talked about time, saying that it passed faster and faster as a person got older. I agreed with him. When you were a kid, a year seemed an eternity, he said. Then he asked me, "Did you ever consider what time must be like for a ghost?"

I shook my head. No, I hadn't given that notion much thought.

He said that for a ghost it was just the opposite. Time passed quickly for a new ghost, but time was slow for a ghost who had been a ghost for a while. Time got slower and slower until there was no time at all.

"No time?" I said.

"No time."

I nodded. I noted that he was drinking water.

When the electricity suddenly (and unexpectedly) went out in the middle of the afternoon, people looked around, their mouths hanging open. Then a lady said very matter-of-factly, "The ghosts are still here."

⊶ *Chapter 8* ⊷

NOPE, NOT A TRANSFORMER

I was a skeptic from the start.

Then the evidence began to accumulate, and explaining or rationalizing it all away became more and more difficult—and, finally, impossible.

⊶ ⊷

On the evening of June 7, 2008, Rebecca and I welcomed to our home a team of paranormal investigators from Louisiana Spirits, a branch of TAPS, the paranormal investigators featured on the SyFy television show *Ghost Hunters*.

When they contacted us about doing an investigation, the Louisiana Spirits (LaSpirits) spokesperson promised they would be as objective and scientific as possible. They would use infrared cameras, digital voice recorders, and devices to measure electrical activity and temperatures. They did not use psychics, and they were cautious about placing a lot of value on any "personal experiences" they might have because of the subjectivity of such experiences.

Rebecca and I gave the six investigators a tour of the house. We talked about the stories we had heard from townspeople and read in books and on the Internet, as well as about what we had personally witnessed. We told them about seeing a second Jacob—or somebody or some *thing* that looked like Jacob—and about the family friend who thought they saw Rebecca in an upstairs window although Rebecca was actually downstairs. They explained that what we apparently had was a doppelganger, an entity that manifested itself by pulling energy from a living individual. It made sense to me that, if an entity was going to use a person's energy to manifest, the entity might look something like the living person. Although the theory was interesting, it seemed too much like an episode of *The Twilight Zone,* and I was still holding out for another explanation.

The investigators brought their equipment into the house and began setting up. They placed cameras in several rooms, and red extension cords were strung all over. They put their monitors on folding tables in the hallway on the second floor and set out battery-operated digital audio recorders. They walked around the house with K2 or EMF (electromagnetic field) devices and thermometers to get base-line readings of electrical activity and temperatures. They seemed pretty excited. After all, no paranormal team had ever done an investigation in the famous Allen House, and they wanted to see whether there was anything to the stories that spanned a half century. Maybe, they could capture evidence of para-

LaSpirits

normal activity. Maybe, they could do some debunking, they said.

But debunking was not in the cards.

Rebecca and I were not sure what the protocol was for having a paranormal investigation conducted. All we knew was what we had observed watching shows like *Ghost Hunters*. It seemed that the homeowners usually left, so we thought LaSpirits might want us out of the way. We planned to go out to dinner and to a late-night movie. The kids were all spending the night with friends of theirs.

As the team members were setting up, one of the investigators felt an electrical shock when she walked into the downstairs bathroom. It was the bathroom we always described as "the creepy bathroom," the one Jacob wouldn't use and the cat wouldn't enter. She asked whether we had ever experienced just walking in there and feeling an electrical shock. We said no.

Another investigator sniffed at the air and asked whether we ever smelled cigar smoke. We said we often did, especially on the first floor, in all kinds of weather and at all times of day. It seemed to come and go. He said he'd first noticed it in the attic and then the smell seemed to follow him as he walked around the house.

Near nine o'clock, they were ready to turn out all the lights and get started. As Rebecca and I prepared to leave and started down the servants' staircase to exit the house from the side door, Rebecca said loudly for all the investigators to hear, "We're leaving! The house is all yours!"

As I descended the stairs, there was a sudden strange feeling in the air, like a static charge. I felt lightheaded and asked Rebecca to drive. I thought, *I need to eat something.*

As we were pulling out of the driveway, I looked at the carriage house and said to Rebecca that maybe the investigators should have set up a camera in there since it was supposed to be a site of some activity. She held out her cell phone to me and said I could call the investigators and make that suggestion.

I said, "No, they can do that when they come back."

"Why would they come back?"

I shook my head. "I don't know. I just have a feeling—"

Then her cell phone rang.

We were no more than two blocks from the house. She listened for a moment and then said into her phone, "All the power? It *all* went out?" She listened. "Okay. We're on our way back."

When we got back to our house, it was totally dark, although our neighbors all had lights on.

The lead investigator explained that just as he was saying, "Lights out. Let's get started," there was a tremendous crash outside, and the backyard lit up with sparks and blue lightning. Then the house went black.

In the backyard, we discovered a large tree branch had fallen across our power line, which lay on the ground. The force of the falling branch on the power line had also ripped the electrical breaker box from the house.

The weather that night was hot, clear, and calm. There was no rain, no wind, and not the slightest breeze. Yet a branch had fallen off a large, seemingly healthy tree—and it just happened to fall on our power line as the lead investigator was saying, "Let's get started."

In addition, one of the investigators received a text message at the exact moment the branch fell. It read: "Urgent. I am watching you." She didn't know who sent the message. The number was unfamiliar. She guessed it was sent by a neighbor of hers in Louisiana, but still, the eeriness of the timing was not diminished.

Rebecca called the electric company, and we all waited outside in the driveway in the hot night for a repair crew to show up.

The investigators left their battery-operated audio recorders running for a while and hoped to still do the investigation, but after a couple of hours of waiting for the power to be restored, we all realized that the electricity was not going to be back on any time soon. In the dark, the members of LaSpirits packed up their equipment and told us they would return on June 28 and try again.

Several hours later, I went into the house to turn off the thermostats so that a power surge wouldn't damage them when the electricity got turned back on. As I expected, the house was very hot; however, when I entered the front parlor, where both sets of double French doors were wide open and letting in the hot summer air, I got goose bumps on my arms and legs. The room was downright chilly. I walked outside, and my arms were still covered with goose bumps. I showed them to Rebecca.

"What happened to you?" she asked.

"I wish I knew."

෴ ෨෧

Between June 7 and June 28, the investigators analyzed the few recordings they had. In the short time they were in the house, they had picked up three EVPs on battery-operated recorders. One EVP was captured in the dining room. What sounded like a man's muffled and gruff voice said, "Hello." An EVP picked up in the front parlor, the room I had found to be chilly on the hot night, was of a whispery female voice very distinctly saying, "Okay … okay." This EVP was so clear that it was hard to believe a living person standing next to the recorder wasn't speaking, yet the voice represented the injection of a third person into a room that only two investigators occupied at the time.

By far, the most provocative of the three EVPs was recorded on the second-floor landing right after the electricity went out and as the investigators were commenting on the "weirdness" of the power outage and speculating as to what had happened. One investigator said, "It must have been a transformer." In the midst of the investigators' talking, a whispery female voice (the same one as in the parlor, it seemed) said, "Not a transformer." Then two or three seconds later, somewhat fainter, the voice repeated, "Not a transformer."

And the investigator who received a text message from a neighbor saying "Urgent: I am watching you"? The neighbor claimed he didn't send it.

∽∾ ∾∽

When Louisiana Spirits returned on the evening of June 28 and commenced their investigation, Rebecca and I stayed at the house. We had once again sent the kids to the houses of friends of theirs, but Rebecca insisted that she and I stay— she didn't want anything else broken. She was convinced that our leaving the house to the investigators on the first occasion had upset the spirits.

For my part, I was still not completely convinced of anything. A part of me continued to resist the idea that Rebecca and I and our children were living with ghosts.

On June 28, 2008, no trees fell. Nothing blew up, but plenty went on.

In the second-floor hallway, Rebecca and I sat and watched the monitors with two LaSpirits team members. I was impressed with the investigators' seriousness and professionalism. They weren't like some of the silly ghost hunters I'd seen on television who screamed at every creak of a floorboard and saw a trapped soul in every dust mote and followed around a spastic "psychic" who always made quick contact with spirits that had invariably met some grisly demise when they were still flesh-and-blood mortals. Rebecca commented about one TV ghost hunter: if the guy saw a rat he'd claim it was a *ghost* rat; if he saw a cockroach, he'd claim it was a *ghost* cockroach. The Louisiana Spirits investigators never jumped to quick conclusions. They studied, tested, and challenged all evidence.

They dismissed anomalies that could be logically explained. For instance, several orbs appeared on most of the eight monitor screens, but the investigators explained that orbs were usually just dust particles or insects.

However, even with the LaSpirits investigators' inclination to explain away events, some interesting and difficult-to-explain things happened from early on in that first full investigation.

In the front parlor, an investigator got some spikes on her EMF meter. Such a spike could be an indication of paranormal activity, she explained, but she could find no logical explanation, like a breaker box or an electrical outlet. This was the parlor where an EVP had been recorded three weeks before, the parlor that had been downright cold in an otherwise hot house, and where our antique Victrola sometimes spun on its own.

Investigators took photos of a blue mist in the doorway of the dining room and of a white mist drifting through the master bedroom suite. They also recorded video of a tiny gauzy-looking object spiraling upward from floor to ceiling in the master bedroom. The spiraling thing that was neither dust nor an insect was freaky. It was like a living thing fleeing when an investigator entered the room with a video camera.

An EMF meter left on the floor of the master bedroom blinked its red lights several times during the night, usually whenever Ladell was mentioned.

In the third-story turret, an investigator asked whether Allen Bonner was present, in response to which she immediately heard—and recorded—a young male voice saying, "Sure." When she asked the question and got the answer, I was watching the monitor that showed the south turret room. I saw her jump.

Around two in the morning, the LaSpirits team packed up their equipment. As they made their final sweep through the house to make sure they weren't leaving any equipment behind, Rebecca said, "You guys look ready for bed."

"I'll be asleep as soon as my head hits the pillow," one of them replied.

"Me, too," another said.

A few weeks later we learned they had gone to their motel and had stayed up the rest of the night. They had randomly started playing some of their audio recordings on the way to the motel and were so intrigued, excited, and surprised by what they heard that they couldn't sleep until total exhaustion hit them—in the bright morning.

∽ ∾

The LaSpirits investigators came back to the Allen House on July 23, 2008, to reveal and discuss all their findings with Rebecca and me. They prefaced their findings by explaining that, typically, if they recorded any kind of evidence at all, they might get one or two EVPs and not necessarily clear ones. At our house on the night of June 28, they had gotten *several* EVPs.

They started playing them on a laptop. Hearing the recorded voices—voices that belonged to no living person who was in the house at the time, voices that apparently belonged to the dead—sent chills down my spine. I saw Rebecca shiver a few times, too. To make sure I didn't have any enemies among unseen entities, I felt the impulse to blurt out, "You know, Ladell seemed to be a really nice person! Smart! Sweet! Nice as can be! She really was!"

The investigators played one EVP after another. "How many of these things do you have?" I asked.

The investigator turned the laptop so that I could see the screen, which was crowded with files. "I'm not sure," she said. "Each has a file name, but I haven't counted them all."

After I listened to all of them again the next day on the CD the investigators gave us, I added them up. By my count—not including questionable clips of indistinct sounds that some listeners might interpret as moans or sighs—the investigators had recorded forty-one EVPs. Yes: forty-one.

The investigators and Rebecca and I discerned what seemed to be at least six different voices.

The male voices included the young man who said, "Sure." Then later, responding to some teasing from an investigator who said, "Scared, scared of two women in here," the same voice said, shyly (it seemed to me), "No, I'm not."

In a different clip, a male voice spit out, "Christ!" It sounded like a curse.

A voice that sounded like an older man said, "Allen."

In response to a string of questions from one of the investigators, a child said, "Be quiet."

The woman who said on the occasion of the first and abbreviated investigation "Okay" and "Not a transformer" did a lot of talking during the second investigation. Some of her words seemed to be interactive, that is, in response to something an investigator was saying or doing, as when she said, "Not a transformer." At other times, her words seemed out of context, suggestive of a residual haunting.

In response to an investigator saying, "Move this table," the female voice said, "Help me." On other clips, she said, "It was justified"; "Not my eyes"; "I just lied"; "Michael ... Michael." A female voice, possibly this same one, responded, "Yeah," when an investigator asked, "Are you the one who made the tree fall on the power line?"

Responding to an investigator who stated: "The spirits in this house are very loving," an older-sounding female said, "They are."

The younger female also distinctly said, "Walter," as Rebecca was telling investigators in the master bedroom that, in addition to the three daughters, the Allens had a son who died in infancy. It was as though the ghost wanted to add that information—the name of the son—to the conversation.

A female voice distinctly, and with defiance, said, "No!" in the master bedroom in the midst of Rebecca recounting to investigators the chronology of Allen family deaths.

While Rebecca talked about the suicide of the man in the Hotchkiss house, saying: "His girlfriend broke up with him and apparently he just couldn't get over it," a female voice injected, somewhat shrilly, "She killed him!"

Chapter 9

"THE MOST HAUNTED HOUSE IN AMERICA"

Now, when people asked me if the house was still haunted, I no longer grinned and shrugged. I no longer said, "Not that I know of," or "Who really knows about these things?"

When I got that question, I simply answered, "Yep."

Rebecca, our kids, and I were sitting in the breakfast room one afternoon having a meal when the door of the nearby cabinet, a piece of furniture original to the house, unlatched itself and opened. I guess we had gotten used to certain things because we all looked at each other and then went right on eating.

When I would look up from the yard or driveway at the north attic window (the panes of which were designed to look like a big snowflake) and thought I saw a face, I no longer automatically dismissed it as just a reflection or shadow.

One evening as I sat on the sofa outside the master bedroom, I noticed that the door would open several inches and

The Cabinet

then close. It happened at least four times. At first, I assumed our cat was playing with the door. Then I noticed the cat sleeping at the other end of the sofa. No windows were open. No air-conditioning was on. The door opened and closed one more time. I got up to see whether somebody was doing it. No one was around. After my inspection, the door stopped opening and closing.

Often, under all different kinds of weather conditions and in different locations, we continued to smell cigar smoke.

Rebecca would be watching television and feel something tug her hair.

Although we were not aware of further doppelganger activity (sightings of our son Jacob in places where he could not possibly be) Rebecca and I did note that Jacob seemed strange at times. At least twice, we remarked to him on his moodiness or gloomy disposition and asked where our happy, loving Jacob was. He had responded, "I'm not Jacob anymore." With great relief, we would find him back to normal just a few minutes later. At other times, he would demonstrate an almost obsessive interest in broad comedy and would assail us with corny jokes, which were oddly old-fashioned—"Why does a chicken cross the road?" for example. The jokes very much reminded me of Allen Bonner's attempts at humor.

◈ ◈

One afternoon, Rebecca was in our dressing room on the second floor and heard what sounded like the heavy footsteps of a large man striding across the attic floor. She was so certain someone was in our attic that she propped a chair under the doorknob of the door leading to the attic staircase and called me at work. By the time I got home, she hadn't heard the footsteps for a while. When I went up to the attic, no one was there. Nothing was disturbed as far as I could tell. The windows were closed. There was no sign whatsoever that anyone had gotten in. Someone would find it impossible to access the attic from the outside of the house unless they had a very long ladder or a power lift.

One day, Rebecca and Joshua and some other kids from Rebecca's film school were downtown at the municipal building shooting footage for a short film about children "Ghost Busters" who were on their way to seek help from the mayor in capturing some ghosts. A couple of police officers stood by watching the filming, and when the shoot was finished, one of the officers started telling Joshua and Rebecca that there was a *real* haunted house in Monticello, that his uncle, who was a police officer back in the sixties and seventies, used to get called to the house all the time because of noises in the attic. "He was scared to death to go to that place," he said. "Uncle John said he'd shake in his boots. He wasn't afraid of bank robbers or murderers, but he was real scared of those ghosts at the Allen House."

Rebecca said to Joshua, "Tell him where you live."

༄ ༄

In addition to our own experiences, guests sometimes claimed to see the apparition of a woman. We had guests who left the house suddenly because of what they merely sensed or felt. People told us they saw faces at the windows and that the faces were not ours or our children's.

I spent time thinking about the experiences of former residents. One of the most provocative ghost stories was that of three young girls playing in the foyer. I had recently learned about different kinds of hauntings from my newfound interest in ghost-hunter TV shows, and I wondered whether the three young girls could represent a residual haunting, an event from the past that replayed repeatedly, maybe at a certain time and under certain conditions—an occasion in the lives of the three Allen daughters somehow imprinted on the house.

I figured an alternative explanation might be grounded in the theory that whatever happened to us in the afterlife was what we expected or desired. If childhood was the happiest time in the lives of the Allen daughters, then perhaps that was the period of life they had chosen to occupy for eternity. Such a theory might also explain sightings of a boy. Could Allen Bonner's preference be for eternal childhood? But his EVPs didn't sound like those of a little boy. The Allen Bonner EVPs were those of a young man.

Maybe the children were not the Allen girls at all or Allen Bonner, but the children of servants or children from an earlier time when schools occupied the site. I still wondered about Houston Meredith, whose tombstone I had found in the carriage house wall.

ॐ ॐ

In 1949, Caddye Allen told people she sealed the master-bedroom suite as a memorial to her daughter. Many town residents came to believe she sealed it because she was scared—because she had seen and/or heard Ladell in there and thought she could lock a ghost in a suite of rooms. When new owners removed the locks from the doors of the master-bedroom suite in 1986, they found the suite eerily preserved as it had been Christmas night 1948. Among the items in the room was a plate—original Allen family china—the plate from which Ladell ate her last meal. Also, according to the Internet articles and several write-ups in books, the new owners discovered on a closet shelf a bottle of mercury cyanide.

One of our visitors after the Louisiana Spirits investigations was a man whose aunt had lived in the house in the 1970s. He said his aunt had the house to herself most of the time because the property manager had a terrible time attracting and retaining tenants. He showed us several photographs he had taken when he visited his aunt at the Allen House. One of photos was of the upstairs hallway. The padlocks on the doors of the master-bedroom suite were visible. Also present in the photo was a large, solid orb next to the transom window of the master bedroom. He gave us a copy of the photo, and the next time we had a paranormal investigator in the house, we showed it to her. The investigator explained that, if the picture had been taken with a digital camera, the orb might be dismissed as dust or moisture, but since it was taken long before digital cameras existed, the orb and its location suggested the presence of a spirit.

When we told the man that we would love to talk with his aunt if she still lived in Monticello, he said that she had died in her early forties. She had injured herself in a fall on the old back steps and her health was never the same afterward. He added that, when his aunt was near death, she said the Allen House had killed her.

ನಿಲ ೧ಶ

One day as I was doing Internet research, I stumbled upon a mention of the Allen House I had not seen before. The website bestandworst.com was conducting an informal poll to determine "The Most Haunted House in America." There were eighty houses listed on the ballot, and of course, the Allen House was one of them. It had quite a few votes. The ballot was open for several months yet, and every few weeks I would check it. The Allen House was always right up there with the Winchester House in California, the Myrtles Plantation in Louisiana, and the Lizzie Borden House in Massachusetts. When the ballot closed, the number one haunted house in America was the Allen House.

∽◦ ◦∽

Throughout the fall of 2008, Allen Bonner (or somebody) kept moving items in the house. A small glass light shade in the children's bathroom ended up sitting upright on the floor across the room. No one would admit to removing it from the light fixture. In the same bathroom a week earlier, a light bulb suddenly exploded for no apparent reason. A week after the glass light shade got moved, Rebecca walked into that bathroom and, for a moment, saw legs—just trouser-clad legs, she said—take a stride across the floor and then dissipate.

Overnight, a five-dollar-bill on the back of the toilet tank in the kids' upstairs bathroom made its way, somehow, to the kitchen table downstairs. And, somehow, the TV in the kitchen got turned on.

Was Allen Bonner still being a prankster? Rebecca said that she often heard a young male voice speak her name. Sometimes she heard the voice when she was working in the yard and listening to music on her iPod. Eerily, the music would stop for an instant; she'd hear her name; then the music would recommence.

One work week, I found a broken glass in the kitchen each morning. The glass might be in the sink or it might be sitting on a counter, broken for no explainable reason during the night. The last item that got broken that week—the climax to the glass-breaking frenzy of somebody or *something*—

was the coffee carafe. We found it on the counter in pieces as if it had simply exploded.

Around this same time, we met a woman who had worked for the owners in the early 1990s, when they had a gift shop. She said that things really did get moved and broken in the shop, often overnight, but sometimes in the middle of the day, too. She would leave the shop for a few minutes, and when she returned, some little knickknack or a China tea cup or a pad of receipts would have been moved from a shelf to a table, or from one end of a table to the other end, or it might be on the floor.

Rebecca set up her camera a few times in a deliberate attempt to capture video evidence of paranormal activity in the kitchen. The camera inevitably would turn off (or got turned off by something) almost as soon as Rebecca left the room. Or it would stay on for a while, then shut itself off, then turn itself back on, maybe hours later. She never had that problem when she was recording special events at the house, or making home movies of our family.

∽∞ ∞∾

In January 2009, Rebecca and I discovered new information about Allen Bonner—newspaper pieces by him and about him, a college yearbook picture of him, and his death certificate. Then one morning, Rebecca saw a dark-haired figure peeking around a corner at her.

I had just awoken our ten-year-old son, Joshua, in his room and come around that corner. Rebecca asked me whether Joshua had followed me out of his room. I said yes because I thought he had—I was certain he had because I had felt him behind me. A little later that morning, Rebecca asked Joshua why he'd peeked at her from around the corner and then pulled back quickly. He said he hadn't. He said he didn't leave his room for a good ten minutes after I woke him up. He had lain in bed for a few minutes and then got dressed before he left his room.

Rebecca's response was, "I didn't think it was you, because the person I saw didn't have a face." Like the man in the big hat, this smaller figure had no facial features. Unlike the man in the hat, this figure was not like a shadow but was three-dimensional.

✎ Chapter 10 ✐

"THEY WOULD REVEAL US"

On January 31, 2009, less than a week after the figure followed me down a short hallway and peeked around a corner at Rebecca, Louisiana Spirits returned to the Allen House to perform another investigation. Convinced that the house was haunted, they were eager to see whether the house was more active or less active in cold weather and to try to gain more information about who the spirits were and how they felt about their existences as ghosts.

The investigators were also eager to see what a new tool, the PEAR REG-1 unit "for detection of anomalous consciousness," might contribute to their attempts to acquire evidence of paranormal activity. "REG" stands for "Random Event Generator." I can't hope to explain the PEAR REG-1 adequately, at least not for a scientist. As I understand it, the device was developed by physicists at Princeton University in the 1960s to measure atomic decay. Paranormal investigators with some knowledge of physics discovered that the device was useful to ghost hunters because, by chance, it detected a human presence at a sub-atomic level.

The way it works is this: investigators set up the program on a laptop computer in a room and then leave the room for at least a half hour. When they return they can see whether the graph created by the program shows any anomalies.

The LaSpirits team member using the PEAR REG-1 first tried it out in the attic. He jogged downstairs with his laptop and excitedly told Rebecca and me that the readings he had just gotten in the south turret room were off the chart. He showed us the laptop screen, and the line providing data about human consciousness had, literally, gone off the chart.

He tried it in the master bedroom, the toy room, and then in the enclosed second-story porch. Downstairs, he tried it in the dining room, the parlor, the library, and the kitchen. The results he got suggested that in more than half of the rooms, there was a human presence although no living human being was in the area of the device during the testing period.

One of the other investigators had a personal experience at the bottom of the attic stairs. A man's voice whispered close to her ear, "This way." She had also felt something touch her. The touch was like a caress.

During the same investigation, one of the EVPs recorded in the attic was of a female saying, "Help me." Rather than a plea for help, it seemed as though the spirit mimicked an investigator who said to a team member, "Help me with this," in reference to setting up a camera. What made this possible mimicking truly freaky was that the spirit said her "Help me" *before* the investigator said his.

This incident was similar to something that had happened to me a few weeks before. I had recorded the same female voice in the attic when Rebecca and I had an EVP session of our own. Sitting in the south turret room, I asked, "Do you like it here?" When I played the recording, the female voice said, "I don't like it here," *before* I asked the question. She had apparently anticipated the question, or she had read my mind. Or maybe the gaunt man at the reunion party for the class of 1955 was right: time moved at a different pace for ghosts.

∽ ∾

The daughter of the woman who owned the house in the late 1980s e-mailed Rebecca one Sunday, and they carried on a brief correspondence. The woman recalled what it was like to live in the house with her parents her first year of college, how eerie it was. She had explored the attic a couple of times and had a box full of love letters from Boyd Bonner, Ladell's ex-husband, but she hadn't looked at them since she was a college student twenty-some years earlier. She wondered whether she even knew what she had done with the letters after several moves. Rebecca and I were envious of such a find and couldn't imagine losing track of those fascinating historical documents.

One of the theories about Ladell's motive for committing suicide was that a lover—a soldier at the World War II prisoner-of-war camp for Italian soldiers just outside of Monticello—had abandoned her at the end of the war. Since the war ended in 1945 and Ladell didn't kill herself until three and a half years later, I was always skeptical of the theory. The idea of the existence of letters from lovers of Ladell fascinated Rebecca and me, however, and we speculated that such letters might illuminate Ladell's motive for taking her life.

During the January 31, 2009, LaSpirits investigation, Rebecca was sitting in the master bedroom, telling the team members about the Boyd Bonner letters and wondering out loud whether there might be other letters hidden somewhere. A digital audio recorder was running at the time, and when the recording of the conversation was played, a startlingly loud female voice (over Rebecca's mention of letters) said, "They would reveal us." It's the loudest EVP anyone has yet recorded in the Allen House. Incidentally, Rebecca was sitting directly below the spot where the letters that would reveal Ladell's reason for wanting to die were hidden in the attic floor, yet to be discovered.

THE TALE OF LADELL

The Arkansan song-writer and performer Lisa Coon frequently tells the story behind the composition of her regionally well-known and prize-winning ballad "The Tale of Ladell."

In 1987, Lisa was singing in clubs at night and working as a house painter by day. The new owners of the Allen House, who had purchased it the year before from the widow of Karl Leidinger, Jr., asked Lisa to give them an estimate on painting the exterior.

The middle-aged woman who owned the house with her husband—I'll call her Patricia—led Lisa upstairs to a window in the master bedroom that allowed Lisa to climb out onto the porch roof to inspect the condition of the shingles on the south turret and its window frames. She stood there on the porch roof awhile, looking things over. The house would be challenging with its height and elaborate architectural details, but she thought she could do the job. Then she suddenly got the feeling someone was watching her, and when she looked at the ground below, she saw staring up at her a long-haired, solid black cat with yellow-orange eyes "as big as quarters." Not sure why exactly, she got a very uncomfortable feeling from the cat, and she hurried back through the window and into the master bedroom.

Patricia showed her around some more and began telling her of all her "encounters" in the house. The new owner was apparently always eager to talk about "her" ghosts.

When they walked into a room that had recently been painted a light blue, Patricia rubbed the wall and said to Lisa, "Ladell likes this color. It soothes her. She has been very calm since I painted it this color." Patricia added that she and her husband tried to do things to the house that would please Ladell and the other spirits, that when they did things that made the spirits uneasy, there was more activity.

One night she and her husband both awoke for no apparent reason and immediately got out of bed and went to the door of their bedroom, the master bedroom. At the same time, their daughter had awoken and was standing in the doorway of her room across the hall. Then they all looked in the same direction and saw a ghostly female figure floating down the stairs.

During this tour of the house, Lisa kept thinking about the black cat with the big eyes, and she couldn't shake the feeling that she was being watched. When Lisa finally mentioned the cat, Patricia said she didn't have one.

All the way home, Lisa tried to analyze the feelings she had experienced in the house and to process the owner's stories of paranormal activity.

Early the next morning, Lisa had a nightmare about the Allen House. She was standing on an incredibly tall ladder, painting the four-story south turret, and then it was as though someone pushed the ladder away from the house. She started falling backwards in slow motion, helpless to save herself. She awoke, her heart pounding, with the compulsion to start writing. Immediately, she got out of bed and she didn't stop writing until a song was completed. She said that as soon as she started playing the song on her guitar, she felt as though she had played the song "a million times before."

She was pleased with the eerie and somber ballad full of heartache, but she had no desire to return to the Allen House. She called Patricia and told her she would not be able to do any painting for her.

ॐ ॐ

On the morning of August 22, 2009, a Saturday, I woke up feeling very glad I didn't have to go to work. It had been a rough week as the university geared up for the start of a new academic year, and I looked forward to the weekend at home. There were all kinds of home-improvement projects for me to work on that sunny Saturday morning, or I could just relax. I could watch a movie, read something, play professional wrestling with the boys (I was "The Dean of Disaster"), or spend time with Rebecca. But for some reason, I felt compelled to "treasure hunt" in the attic.

I hadn't done any treasure hunting up there in several months, in large part because I felt sure I had probably found all I was going to find. Resisting the urge, I told myself I had plenty of things to do that morning other than stir up dust in the attic.

But I couldn't shake the compulsion. It was as though I had a voice in my head—a strange voice not entirely my own—saying, "Go to the attic. You'll find something interesting."

"I'll be wasting my time," I said back to the voice in my head. "I'll stir up dust. I'll get dirty. The dust will trigger my allergies."

But I loved finding little artifacts—even if just buttons, thread spools, or pieces of old broken glass. I had a hunch I'd find something that day, so I decided that I might as well spend a little time hunting.

At about eight-thirty, I went up the attic stairs. I had grabbed a flashlight on my way because the strange voice in my head said, "You'll need a flashlight."

I did not aimlessly wander around the huge attic. Instead, I felt immediately drawn to a spot at the edge of the south turret—a small gap between floorboards. I had stepped over the gap dozens of times and had casually looked down at it many times. Seeing nothing but darkness, I had thought nothing of it.

Now I knelt down over the small space between the floorboards and shined my flashlight through it. At first, I didn't see anything, and I started to get up. Then I felt as though someone's hand gently pressed on my shoulder, urging me to look again. I took another look. This time I saw what looked like a small roll of brown butcher paper. Old pieces of wall paper and old newspaper were pretty common in the attic, so a glimpse of old brown paper didn't strike me as particularly interesting. But I felt that gentle nudge again. The nudge of a small hand, one that could probably easily reach into the space.

But my hand was large and it wouldn't be easy. Nonetheless, I reached a couple of fingers through the opening in the floor, got hold of the edge of the brown paper, and gently tugged.

What slipped through that crack was a five-inch-by-nine-inch brown envelope. It was not sealed, and when I lifted up the flap, I saw inside several small white envelopes. I pulled one out. The typed address was "L. A. Bonner, Box 144, Monticello, Ark." There was no return address.

In a moment of supreme denseness, I wondered who "L. A. Bonner" was.

Then I caught my breath because I knew I held something belonging to Ladell Allen Bonner.

The post mark was from 1948. At first, I felt disappointed that the envelope wasn't from earlier in the twentieth century. Then I realized this envelope was from the last year of Ladell's life. I opened it and pulled out a sheet of stationery— a typed letter. It started, "My dear." It was signed "Love, P."

There I was, on my knees on the attic floor, waiting to wake up—I assumed I was dreaming.

When I convinced myself I wasn't dreaming, I peered through the small space in the floor again. My flashlight illuminated something else down there that I couldn't reach. I hurried downstairs to get a hammer. Rebecca said, "What are you doing up in the attic?" I don't think I answered her. I found a hammer and ran back upstairs.

It was already hot in the attic. Sweat ran down my face and my T-shirt was soaked. I inserted the claws of the hammerhead at the edge of the floorboard and pulled. The floorboard started to grudgingly give. The nails screeched.

I shivered as if I had just been enveloped in a cold wind. The floor board came up, and I pushed it aside, and there beneath the floor, covered by the dust of sixty-one years, were more brown envelopes and a few stray white ones scattered about, along with an empty Puerto Rican rum bottle.

I pulled letters from envelopes at random and quickly read about half a dozen. Nothing made much sense to me at first. Most of the letters had postmarks of places far from Monticello, Arkansas. Some were from Minneapolis. Others were from South Dakota and North Dakota. They started "Dear Dell," "Dear Miss Allen," "Dear Sweetheart," "Sweetie," "My Darling." They were all signed "P." This "P" guy talked about business trips, about planning hunting trips, about being on hunting trips, about his hope that Harry Truman would lose the presidential election. Finally, he always told Ladell that he loved her, that he wished he could see her soon, that he wished he could at least call her long distance, and that he would write again soon. These first letters I read were all from the autumn of 1948, the last autumn of Ladell's life.

I started arranging the envelopes by postmark date. Then I counted them. There were eighty-three. They weren't all from "P". Two were from 1945, one of which was from Ladell's ex-husband, Boyd Bonner, and the other from a male acquaintance Ladell had apparently met on a trip to New Orleans and whom her sister, Lonnie Lee, disapproved of. The writer said more than once that he was very sorry about the way Ladell's sister felt about him and that he was sorry about the trouble he had caused Ladell. The rest of the letters were all written in 1948, starting in March. A few of the

Finding Letters

The Letters

letters were from a woman in Hot Springs, Arkansas. Others were from a woman in Helena, Arkansas. One was from a woman in Stillwater, Minnesota. One was from Nova Scotia. One from Newton Center, Massachusetts. Most were from Minneapolis, from the "P" man. Inside several of the envelopes from "P" were letters (or in most cases fragments of letters) that Ladell had written to him and that he apparently had returned.

I finally went downstairs with a couple of the letters, and playfully hiding them behind my back, I said to Rebecca, "Guess what I found in the attic."

"I hope it's money. Did you find Joe Lee Allen's stash of gold?"

"Better," I said. And I held out the letters to her.

Rebecca stared at them. Finally, she said, "These are to Ladell!"

"Yeah! And there are about eighty of them!" I watched her jaw drop and her eyes pop wide.

"This is so cool!"

"They're mostly from some guy who was madly in love with her."

Rebecca asked, "What's his name? Is it 'Michael'? Like from that EVP?"

"No. I don't know his name yet. It starts with a 'P.'"

I told Rebecca how I had felt compelled to go to the attic and was immediately drawn to the place where the letters were hidden.

"Why did *you* get to find them?" Rebecca asked. "I want to find something like that."

"I guess Ladell likes me better," I joked.

౿ఎ ౿ఎ

I spent the rest of that Saturday in the attic, organizing the letters and reading them. The earliest letter (written March 19, 1948) revealed "P's" full name: Prentiss Hemingway Savage.

Starting with that first letter and reading them chronologically, I witnessed the onset of a love affair, the first flirtations and hesitations, the evolution toward more confident expressions of affection, then declarations of passion, of dedication, and the insistence that the promises being made would never be broken ... then the frustrations, the disappointments, the sorrow, and the downward spiraling into deep depression.

Knowing how this love affair was going to end, I looked up from a letter written in early July 1948 and said aloud to the dark, fire-scorched rafters of the attic, "Oh, Ladell. I am so sorry."

Rebecca was busy that day preparing for and hosting a friend's teenager's birthday party downstairs. It was a costume party with a Roaring Twenties theme. At one point in the afternoon, I looked up from a letter and saw a beautiful woman coming across the attic toward me. She wore the short hair style of a 1920s flapper and a flapper dress, even the popular round woman's hat of the day with the bill that came down over the eyes forcing the wearer to lift her chin, giving her a somewhat haughty look. Startled, I blinked sweat out of my eyes. The woman disappeared. I blinked again, fast, several times, and she re-appeared but seemed different. The hair wasn't quite the same, the dress a different color, it seemed.

"Honey?" she said.

It was Rebecca. At least the second woman was.

❧ ☙

I was in awe of what had happened to me that Saturday, as well as what I had found. I honestly felt I had been *led* to those letters.

The next morning, Rebecca and I began researching the people who authored the letters and the people who were mentioned in them.

We had known that Martha Anne Jones was Ladell's only niece, Lewie's daughter. What we didn't know the day I found the letters was that, less than two weeks before, Martha had passed away at the age of seventy-nine. She had been the last living person with whom Ladell had had any kind of close relationship. When Ladell was fifty-four, Martha was eighteen. A June 1948 letter from Prentiss mentioned Ladell attending her niece's high-school graduation in Memphis. Prentiss remarked that it must have been a tremendous pleasure for Ladell to witness the graduation of her beloved niece to whom she was so close, having filled the role of mother to a certain extent after Lewie's death when Martha was only fourteen years old.

Some people have suggested to me that I found the letters that Saturday morning because the time was finally right—that Ladell herself was ready to reveal her secrets, to have her story finally told. An interesting theory that I've become convinced is right. I think that Ladell conveyed to Lisa Coon the helplessness she felt in falling in love with Prentiss Hemingway Savage and having no control over the relationship. What Ladell experienced was like falling from a very tall ladder, the inevitable result being death. I think Ladell led me to the letters so the details of her helplessness could finally be revealed.

Chapter 12

THE OWL TRAIN

A couple of nights after I found and read all the letters, I had a vivid dream that didn't seem like a dream at all, but like reality. I could hear background noises in the dream, like the rustle of leaves and the whinny of horses in the distance. I could smell chimney smoke.

In my dream, Prentiss and Ladell were on the porch of the Allen House at night, sitting in shadow on a porch swing (a swing long gone in the real world in the year 2009, except for the big hooks that remain in the porch ceiling). They sat close, Prentiss dressed in a brown pin-striped suit with a stiff white collar and Ladell wearing a dress with a long skirt and puffy sleeves. Even though they were in shadow, it seemed to me that Prentiss' face was very tanned and hers very pale. Her lips were very red.

Behind the parlor windows, Ladell's mother, Caddye, lurked. Prentiss shifted on the swing. He leaned toward Ladell's red lips. And to warn them that she was watching, Caddye dropped a large leather-bound book entitled *Vivilore: A Pathway to Mental and Physical Perfection*, which slammed against the oak floor with resonance. *Vivilore* was not mentioned in any of the letters but made its way into my dream, I'm sure, because I owned a copy of the book, which Rebecca and I kept as a decoration and conversation piece on top of the Victrola in the front parlor. It was published in 1904 as an educational volume for young women, giving them instruction in proper hygiene, proper conduct while courting, proper conduct for a wife, proper conduct for an expectant mother, proper conduct for a mother. The operative word really was "proper." It was just the kind of book that Caddye would have pressed upon her daughters. Caddye herself was quite proper despite her love of parties.

My dream was about the night in February 1913 on which Ladell and Prentiss had their last date before he caught the night train—the "owl train," as he called it—for Tyler, Texas, where a job awaited. Although it was winter, it was a mild night, not unusual in southern Arkansas.

The noise of the dropped book startled Prentiss. He jerked back from Ladell, who giggled at him and then turned toward the parlor windows and frowned at the silhouette of her mother. Ladell was fresh-faced and pretty and not even nineteen years old yet. Twenty-year-old Prentiss was athletic-looking even in his travelling suit.

He pulled out a pocket watch. It was time to go.

They walked south down North Main Street to the train depot, Prentiss carrying his leather grip, the stars hard and sharp, the trees black and skeletal in the winter night. Oddly, I kept hearing thunder.

The train platform was empty except for them. The dining car was dark. Steam hissed somewhere down the track.

He said he would write as soon as he settled into his new job. Ladell didn't speak. She just looked up at him, shivering, and nodded.

Then he stepped aboard, and Ladell stepped back and watched the black owl train snake out of Monticello, Arkansas, its whistle screeching and its white smoke dissipating into the blue night like a ghost. And oddly, thunder clapped. Then Ladell turned away from watching the train disappear into the night. She looked at me (the dreamer) with a blank expression I could not read. It was as if she were in a daze.

Thunder clapped again, and I awoke to a raging storm outside. Rain and hail pelted the windows of the second-story turret where Rebecca and I sleep. Wind howled. I looked at the red numbers of the electric alarm clock on the night stand (it was 2:13), and in that instant, the power went out, and I heard whispered in my ear, "You know."

Except for the small details of the dream, I knew it was all true, because I had read the letters in which Prentiss reminisced about that occasion.

એ ા

The young Prentiss Savage and Ladell Allen were well suited for each other in 1913. I knew from countless old newspaper notices and advertisements and from hundred-year-old legal documents on file at the courthouse that her father was a bank president and had been appointed by a state governor as county treasurer. He owned a livery stable, a hotel, about a third of all the rental property in town, a taxi service, and a horse-drawn rental hearse. From a Hemingway family history (Prentiss' mother was a Hemingway), I learned that Prentiss was descended from physicians and musicians. From the letters I'd discovered, it was clear that he and Ladell had grown up together, had gone to the same parties, had known all the same families. He was muscular, handsome, and a star baseball pitcher; she was petite and pretty.

But Prentiss had to catch that train to Texas—to seek his future and his fortune.

He did write ... for a while. But in his absence Ladell allowed herself to be courted by a tall, light-haired, blue-eyed, hard-drinking Yankee, who had come to Arkansas from Indiana to operate a pool hall, and soon enough Prentiss got word from folks in Monticello that his girl had been stolen.

In November of 1914, Ladell married Boyd Bonner. On her and Boyd's first anniversary, she gave birth to their only child, Elliott Allen Bonner, the "Elliott" part of the baby's name quickly dropped and forgotten, probably because it was a Bonner family name and Ladell's son would have little to do with his father.

As Ladell stated in one of her letters to Prentiss, life with Boyd just didn't work out. Ladell, Boyd, and Allen moved a lot. Boyd kept changing jobs. He was a heavy drinker and a playboy.

After a privileged life of opulence, parties, and vacations, Ladell found adulthood to be a series of trials, heartbreaks, and tragedies—the bad marriage, the divorce, her separation from her son for much of his adolescence, the death of her son when he was only twenty-eight, the death of her younger sister ...

At the end of World War II, in the summer of 1945, just as she was entering her fifties and living in Monticello again,

Ladell's most recent lover, a soldier stationed at the nearby Italian prisoner-of-war camp, left her.

∽ ∾

On March 10, 1948, her fifty-fourth birthday was less than two weeks away. She was living with and caring for her seventy-seven-year-old mother, and despite an active social life, Ladell was lonely and afraid of what lay ahead. She was grieving all she had lost and searching for comfort and hope in newspaper horoscopes and Christian Science.

Then the doorbell rang, and there stood Prentiss Savage.

The boy she should have married in the first place, should have married thirty-five years before, had grown into a fine and impressive man, an oil executive in Minneapolis, and he had suddenly and unexpectedly re-appeared in her life. He was so charming, and he knew just what to say—he told her she was the same Dell he had known in 1913.

In the months that followed, her hope for love and happiness was renewed—and then crushed.

Chapter 13

THE LOVE OF
LADELL'S LIFE

My discovery of the letters was big news in Monticello, Arkansas, and beyond. The state newspaper ran a piece about the house's reputation for paranormal activity, Ladell's suicide, and the discovery of the correspondence, which shed new light upon the suicide and perhaps the haunting. With the lurid headline "A Toxic Affair," the local newspaper ran a full-page, Section-A story with photos. The subheading was "Mystery Solved."

Now we knew why Ladell had committed suicide.

Several comments on the local newspaper's website were from folks who wanted to share their own observations and experiences and opinions regarding the Allen House. A handful of people thought the story tawdry and reproached Rebecca and me for bringing Ladell's secret to light. They thought that Ladell's affair with Prentiss Savage should have been kept a secret to preserve her "reputation" in the community, that the letters should have been destroyed upon discovery. *Odd*, I thought. The only widespread reputation I was aware of was that she was a suicidal alcoholic ghost who had been scaring people for over sixty years. My feeling about the letters was that they gave us tremendous insight into Ladell as a complex human being worthy of our compassion and sympathy and whose fears and needs were not so far removed from those of most of us.

Most people, even people who had never seen the inside of the house, just wanted to state their claims of having seen faces and mysterious flicking lights in the second and third-story windows, of having crossed to the other side of the street whenever they walked past because of the creepy vibes coming from the house, of having heard sensational stories of flying objects and full-body apparitions from people who had been in the house.

A stranger, a middle-aged woman, called me after the newspaper story appeared to tell me that when she was a little girl she used to accompany her electrician father on jobs sometimes, and in the attic of the Allen House they both got so scared hearing noises and seeing strange shadows that they left before he finished the job. Her father told the owners they'd have to find another electrician.

Another woman said she had written a research paper twenty years ago about the Allen House for a high-school class and had always been fascinated with it. She was so fascinated with it that she was hoping I would consider allowing her to live in my attic.

No one in 2009 claimed to have known the living Ladell, not even people well into their eighties or nineties. They only knew of her and remembered the talk at the time of the suicide—people couldn't understand why somebody with so much money would want to kill herself. But, of course, while no one claimed to have known Ladell, some people did claim to have seen her ghost.

Something a lot of people theorized, including several paranormal investigators, was that Ladell would disappear from the Allen House now that her secret was out, that she no longer had a reason to stay.

ᴄᴏ ᴏᴏ

Prentiss Hemingway Savage's personality, background, interests, and values came through quite clearly in the letters he wrote to Ladell.

After he left Monticello in the winter of 1913, he worked in Tyler, Texas, for four years. Then he served as an officer and flew planes in France in 1917–1918 during World War I. What specific horrors he had witnessed in France he shied away from describing to Ladell, but the possibilities could easily have included aerial dogfights, the machine-gun strafing of infantry troops, soldiers blown to pieces by missiles (perhaps while simply sitting in a foxhole), soldiers lost and blind in a sea of mustard gas. The new efficient and impersonal technologies of war had made death a gruesome possibility for men who may never get near their enemy, undermining old-fashioned notions of the glory of hand-to-hand combat, undermining people's belief in a coherent world, in a benevolent and engaged deity overseeing all the activities of man.

There were times and places Prentiss would wish he could forget—Belleau Wood, Soissons, the Champagne, St. Mihiel—

places densely littered with the swollen and dismembered corpses of soldiers.

The forests of France, reduced to the black broken skeletons of a few trees, were silent because there were no birds.

Villages were transformed to smoking timbers and piles of jagged rubble, the bodies of women here and there, their white socks muddied, their feet askew, their long hair tousled by the breeze. And there were the bodies of the children, their limbs tossed wide, like rag dolls.

Surely, what Prentiss experienced in The Great War contributed to the dark vision of life he confessed to have and described to Ladell in abstract terms. He was a "fatalist," he said. Life was hell. The world was "wicked." He paid lip-service to conventional religion and expressed admiration of Ladell's regular church attendance, but he never attended church himself. Any faith he possessed during his relationship with Ladell in 1948 was brief and tenuous.

Indicative of his inclination to be either macabre or morose or both at times, Prentiss wrote of a Filipino who described to him the horrors of the Bataan Death March during World War II:

> *For instance, he said that they would stop about once each day and boil some rice, rather the Japs would, and then serve them right out of the boiler in a scoop right into their bare hands, and of course it was so hot they could not hold it so they dropped it to the ground and then got down and started eating it off the dirty ground. This was just one of the many things, the others so horrible it was unbelievable*

except that you knew it was coming from a person who was truthful.

As someone who shared similar experiences, he had tremendous respect and appreciation for what the veterans of the Second World War had been through:

When I was in Sioux Falls the other day I ran into Joe Foss. You remember him as the big war ace in the Pacific having shot down some 45 or 50 Japs. He was a marine flyer. I knew him only casually but had dinner with him the other night, and after much prodding I got him to talking and what experiences! Seems to me he should be a nervous wreck but instead he appears to have not a nerve in his body. It was interesting, since I was flying with one of our tanker ships the other day as well, and the boy who was my pilot was a hero in Germany with many decorations. Between the two of them I really got a liberal education in how wars are now fought in the air.

Back in the states after World War I, Prentiss did not allow any kind of disillusionment to stifle his ambitions. He was determined to be a wealthy man. He worked hard and made his way up in the oil business. Living in Los Angeles and then Spokane, Washington, during the 1920s, and Butte, Montana, during the 1930s, and then in Minneapolis, he eventually became not only a vice-president with Texaco Oil but also an executive for Ruan Transport Corporation, one of the nation's largest carriers of bulk petroleum products.

He loved golf, fishing, hunting, and attending baseball and football games. His one vice, he claimed, was his work. Despite the stress of it, he loved his job—or at least he claimed he would feel lost without it. He was a man of his time and of his social class, and a product of the segregated South. He referred to women of all ages as "little" and as "girls." He was racially prejudiced. He described himself both as a "gentleman" and as a "wolf." He was a teetotaler. His politics were Republican, and he abhorred the New Deal, labor unions, taxes, government regulations on oil companies, Franklin Roosevelt, and Harry Truman. He never wrote more than one draft of a letter, preferring to type them, usually on his secretary's typewriter on Saturdays and Sundays, or in the evenings. He loved to fly, he told Ladell.

In contrast, Ladell was a liberal Democrat with a profound interest in astrology and a desire to understand the Christian Science faith although she attended the Presbyterian Church of Monticello every Sunday if she was not out of town. She was a "lady," but she did things a lady was not supposed to do. She had a sharp mind for business. She enjoyed baking and playing bridge. She was intelligent, considerate, and eager to please others. She preferred to write her letters in long hand and did multiple drafts, taking great care in how she worded her questions and expressed her fears and affection. But she typed the envelopes, probably out of her paranoia that someone in Prentiss' office would recognize her hand writing as that of a woman. She had a fear of flying, she told Prentiss, that kept her from ever getting on an airplane.

Although he was highly successful as a businessman and derived a lot of pleasure from his work, Prentiss' domestic life was disappointing, even miserable at times. He was married twice, first to a woman named Helen, then to a woman named Helene, a cold woman disliked by his family and who shared none of his interests. In the letters, he referred to Helene with only the initial "H," which was also how he made reference to Hell.

On March 10, 1948, Prentiss, as he described in a letter he wrote later that year, walked up to the Allen House, saying to himself: *I wonder if Dell will be cute like she used to be or if she will be old and weathered.*

Thirty-five years after their last date, Ladell and Prentiss found themselves part of a group going to the horse races in Hot Springs. Prentiss was in Arkansas to visit relatives and a few old friends and to take a break from the fast pace of his life in Minneapolis. He had no idea he would be seeing Ladell Allen, his old flame. He would later speculate that their reunion must have been fated.

He and Ladell and the others in their group shared a raccoon dinner, and although he talked of visiting her in Monticello before he returned to Minneapolis, he was not able to, likely because of his travelling companion: his wife.

FINDING A LITTLE HAPPINESS ALONG THE WAY

Prentiss did, however, write Ladell a letter soon after he returned to Minneapolis:

March 19, 1948.
P. H. Savage
300 Baker Building
Minneapolis 2, Minn.

My dear Dell:
Hope that foursome of yours got back to Monticello in good shape after the races. That's quite a gang you had with you and I liked all of them. Sorry you all did not clean up on the races, but I guess none of us ever do.

We arrived home without mishap and now that I have had time to get some of my business chores worked out, I naturally find myself recalling some of the happenings of the trip south, and one of the highlights was indeed seeing you. It certainly brought back to me many memories of my youth in Monticello. You have changed so very little and I can see why, since your mother too is much like she was when I saw her last. Believe it or not, it was in 1913.

I did enjoy the coon dinner with you. Wasn't that a wonderful dinner with coon, sweet potatoes and black eyed peas all of which are difficult to get here. We Yankees don't seem to appreciate good food.

First time I get over into Wisconsin I have a cheese place that makes up delectable packages and so I'll send you one. Hope you will like it.

It was so nice seeing you again, Dell, and with all good wishes, believe me,

Sincerely,
Prentiss

The "wonderful coon dinner" and the promise to send cheese initiated a food theme in their letters. They seemed to want to nourish each other and give each other pleasure through food. He wanted to send her cheese and pheasants. She wanted to bake him cakes and send him vegetables from her garden. After they spent nearly three weeks together in the coming summer, they had an ongoing private joke about "EAT," a reference to highway billboards about which Ladell had made some remark that delighted Prentiss, a remark apparently full of sexual innuendo.

Ladell responded "promptly" to Prentiss' first letter. He thought her quick reply was "real cute." It was soon apparent that the sparks of their teen-age romance still glowed. Prentiss wrote:

> *It seems so natural to hear from you and I hope you will have no concern over writing. Telling Virginia about hearing from me was perfectly alright and I am sure she will forget it.*
>
> *You certainly are as near the Dell I knew years ago as you could possibly be. I see so little change in you. Dell, you have one outstanding trait and that is you make everyone love you and all of those I talked with told me what a wonderful sweet person you were, how everyone loved you and how you made everyone happy when you were around them. That's the way you were as a girl and I can understand after seeing you again. Keep smiling.*

I wondered who Virginia was, and in my research I easily discovered that she was the daughter of Prentiss' sister, Genevieve. Apparently, Ladell and Virginia were good friends, and Ladell visited her in her recently built home in Monticello. More interesting was the fact that Virginia's home was the rental house with the crooked floors that Rebecca and I and our children lived in when we first moved to Monticello. *That is an eerie coincidence*, I thought. And that house sat on "Allen Street."

The local newspaper story about my discovery of the letters didn't mention the name of the man Ladell had carried on the correspondence and affair with in 1948, but the day after the story ran, Rebecca got a call from the woman who had rented us the house with the crooked floors. She thanked Rebecca for cleaning the rental house so thoroughly when we moved out. Rebecca thought it a little odd that the woman would wait three years to say thanks for cleaning her rental house, but then the lady got to the real point of her call. She said, "The man who wrote those letters was Prentiss Savage, wasn't he? He was my husband's uncle."

Rebecca invited her over to see the correspondence. The woman, who was eighty years old, came to the house a few days later. I spent a couple of hours with her in my library, asking her questions, and she read several of the letters. "Uncle Prentiss" had given her husband his first job, back in 1949. Prentiss attended her wedding in 1950. She recalled him as a distinguished, handsome, and kind "older man." She remarked that she wasn't even twenty years old the first time she met him and that it would have never occurred to her at the time that someone so *old* (he was fifty-six or fifty-seven) would be interested in romance or sex.

Truly poignant for her was getting to hold and read the letters written by Prentiss' sister, Genevieve, whom she had known very well and had been very fond of. Genevieve had known everything about Prentiss and Ladell but had never told a soul. My elderly guest said that Genevieve had simply been that way. Genevieve was no gossip and certainly had no desire to besmirch her brother's reputation or that of her dear friend Dell.

The lady kept shaking her head in awe over this piece of her family history I had discovered in my attic. She said that Prentiss only occasionally brought his wife with him when he visited relatives in Arkansas and that the family knew his marriage was unhappy. There had even been rumors that

Prentiss might be a bit of a wolf, but no one could blame him.

⤶ ⤷

Ladell wasted no time falling in love. In a letter Prentiss received on April 2, Ladell expressed concern that "her feelings" were "wrong" and that their correspondence was "wrong." Prentiss argued in his reply that a person couldn't always "follow the rules," that a person had to try "to find a little happiness along the way." He cited the famous 1920s charismatic evangelist Aimee Semple McPherson as an example of how "even preachers" looked for ways to have a good time:

> *If you feel that you are depriving someone of something by writing me, erase it from your mind because you are not. I can see nothing so terrible about you writing me if you enjoy it and I certainly do not think there is so much wrong with me writing you since I love to do so. You know one can go through life and live up to every law of man and god, and when he dies, an epitaph could be placed at his grave reading "He lived by the rules." But to that should be added—what a life!*
>
> *People go to church to hear the word spoken but did you ever realize that even the preachers look for a little pleasure and happiness along the way. For example when I lived in Los Angeles some years ago Sister Aimee McPherson was in her heyday and visitors coming to the city would want me to take them down to the Four Square Gospel so they could see Aimee. We would go, and there she would be all robed in white gown, a beautiful face and a voice filled with sobs,*

*crying out "come unto me" and be saved etc. Well, you re-
member in all of her sanctity she too felt that life was pretty
drab and she took herself out into the desert and got lost—
you read accounts in the papers. That's all I am doing, trying to find a little happiness along the way and your letters
give me that.*

Aimee Semple McPherson (1890–1944) was the flamboyant and electrifying founder of the International Church of
the Four Square Gospel. On May 18, 1926, she disappeared at
a California beach and was believed drowned. Her devastated
followers held memorial services. Coincidentally, a young
man in her employment had also disappeared. Then on June
23, she turned up in a Mexican town near the Arizona bor-
der, claiming she had been kidnapped and, after finally escap-
ing from her captures, had walked thirteen hours across the
Mexican desert. Mysteriously, however, her shoes showed
no signs of a thirteen-hour trek across the desert, and she
was fully dressed in one of her own outfits despite having
disappeared in a bathing suit, and she was wearing a wrist
watch (a gift from her mother) that she had not even taken to
the beach the day she disappeared. Soon enough, the more
likely truth came out: she had run away with a married lover,
the young man in her employment. Apparently, after a few
weeks, her passion for her lover cooled, and she started to
regret abandoning her religious empire.

Ironically, Prentiss' example of someone who broke the
rules to pursue pleasure—the role model he obviously hoped
Ladell would adopt—had wrecked her personal and profes-

sional lives and eventually died of an overdose of sleeping pills near her fifty-fourth birthday.

Regardless of whether she contemplated the consequences Aimee Semple McPherson had suffered, Ladell was persuaded to "break the rules"—and she continued to write. Still uneasy, however, about how others might interpret the correspondence and where the correspondence might lead, Ladell asked him to destroy her letters, and he agreed to do so:

> *You need have no fear about writing me, dear, because after I memorize what you write I then destroy your letters. I hate to do it but perhaps it is best and after all I promised you I would. I don't feel we are hurting anyone in writing and then too I just love to hear from you – darn it. But you are right in that there is no reason to publish to the world that we write because I presume your friends in Monticello would just have something they could talk about and I would not give them the privilege.*

As I mentioned earlier, in several of Prentiss' envelopes were fragments of her letters—his proof to her that he was not risking the possibility that her letters could be discovered, at least not on his end.

Without doubt, Prentiss, too, was aware of the risk in their corresponding. After all, it was 1948, a time before the cultural and sexual revolution of the 1960s, a time not really so far removed from Victorian attitudes, especially in the South and Midwest. He *was* married, and he and Ladell both were prominent individuals in their communities and therefore attractive subjects for gossip:

> *Yes I thought it best that I stop using stationery with my name on it because there may be someone in the post office with eyes on you and he would not approve, and it might cause just a little fama clamosa [scandal].*

Ladell always typed "personal and confidential" on her envelopes. On later correspondence, along with her post office box number, she put "H. H. Savage" in the sender's space, a ruse to make people in Prentiss' office believe he was receiving mail from his brother, Harry. With the exception of his first one, his letters were always sent to her post-office box. On the days she received a letter, she walked from the post office to the drug store in the next block and sat with a cup of coffee and eagerly, anxiously read. She described her routine and emotions to Prentiss, and he occasionally alluded to them:

> *This letter is getting long and I must spare you. Otherwise you'll never get out of that drug store and away from that coffee …*
>
> *Yes, I am glad that you anxiously await a letter from me and you may be sure that six days waiting at this end of the line is just as long. I am really a very poor correspondent and have never carried one on but I am like an old hound dog looking for coon when it comes to keeping a weather eye on the mail that comes to me. I scan through the stack to see if by chance there might be one from Monticello.*

In this early stage of the correspondence, they wrote each other only once a week. Nonetheless, by the middle of April, they were discussing a way to get together. He frequently traveled on business, and she frequently visited friends in other states or took shopping trips to large cities, so a meeting seemed entirely feasible. Prentiss was eager for a tryst:

I surely would have occasion to plan a business trip anywhere if you were going to be there.

But Memphis would be a bad place for me as I am sure I would run into someone from Helena [where his sister lived] and that would be not so good. I have met so many people over there and while I might not recognize them they surely would be the type to recognize me. Anyway you think it over and when you think you can get away and decide on the place let me know and I'll make my plans accordingly.

If you should show up around any part of the country north of the Mason and Dickson line, I'll find some reason to be there too.

Obviously, Prentiss meant "Dixon" rather than "Dickson." (An interesting Freudian slip, perhaps.)

Several references to Ladell's rose bushes interested me, in part because Rebecca had heard a woman's voice close to her ear on more than one occasion when she was in the yard working with flowers. The voice would say, "My roses."

Prentiss wrote:

Yes, honey, I guess you are a better gardener than I am because my roses are not even started yet and won't be for another four to six weeks, but I have uncovered them and they are not dead and that is something.

On another occasion, Prentiss, who was far more obsessed with golf than he was with gardening, wrote:

Last Sunday I played golf and then went home about four and worked in my flower bed for about two hours, and Monday I could hardly walk. What effort to have a few roses. They better grow abundantly this year or I'll feel like giving up.

With my metal detector one day, I found an old lipstick tube, a tiny tin pillbox, and a 1948 penny under one of the old rose bushes.

co ow

The correspondence with Ladell certainly made Prentiss nostalgic:

You make me homesick for Arkansas when you talk of water melons. We get them here but not like those Old Man Wall used to grow or Babe Cruit. No you never went on the hay rides but I used to be the one that got through the fence and fetched the melons. I got to where I could thump them with my finger and tell immediately whether I should fetch it. What days those were. ... How on earth could you remember me leaving on the Owl for Tyler—but after all you were my last date and I kept you up till shortly before the Owl left as I remember. Thirty five years ago last February—perish the thought—couldn't be.

He seemed to have a particular fondness for a memory connected with baseball and money:

...Every time the Fourth of July comes around I think about 1910. I was quite young and pitching baseball for Blissville Lumber on that day in Crossett. We had gone over there in a special train from Blissville to play the Crossett Lumber Company team and it was quite a good team but we thought we were better. Anyway it was dreadfully hot and we won the game about four to one and then we got on the Special to return to Blissville and of course everyone who worked for the Blissville lumber company was on that train. I got myself well seated and the lumber mill workers started coming around to where I was sitting and handed me anywhere from one to ten dollars, money which they had won betting on Blissville. They thought I had single-handedly won the game, which I had not, but I got the money and when I got to Blissville I took all that money out and put it on the bed and started counting it and I had over three hundred dollars and I thought I was really rich. I had to tell you about this because it is one of the memories of my boyhood I always remember on the Fourth.

For both Prentiss and Ladell, their correspondence represented a recapturing of their youths. Surely, Ladell liked his assurances that time had not touched her beauty. He was very good at transporting her back in time, wiping away her disappointing adulthood, as when he addressed his letters to "Miss Allen."

Throughout May, their correspondence continued to be limited to one letter a week. He wrote on Saturday, and she replied on Monday or Tuesday, depending on which day she received his letter. They continued to try to figure out how to meet up. Prentiss stumbled all over himself trying to accommodate her and lure her to a meeting, so eager was he to see her "in the flesh":

> *If you should decide to go to Indianapolis I could come down there. I get to St. Louis occasionally, Chicago often and if Indiana is your journey's end then I will find a reason to get down that way. I do hope you can come up this way and visit in Stillwater, but if you can't, let me know a little in advance and I'll come and see you. I was in Stillwater the other day and thought of you, remembering that you had told me you might come up. It is an old town, an old lumbering town but it is rather fascinating. They have a lovely hotel there and right across the river is Wisconsin where everyone goes to eat frog legs.*

They continued to share news of their roses. Were they conscious of the symbolism? And they clearly worked at revealing to each other their everyday habits in an attempt to create a greater sense of familiarity and intimacy:

> *I wanted to work in my flower garden this morning but it is raining and so I'll wait. Sunday is a bad day for me to think of flowers because I usually go to the golf club about nine and have breakfast, play, and then do a wee bit of gambling. Isn't that a Christian way to spend Sunday, and*

especially for one who practically grew up in the old Presby-
terian Church there.

… So you can cook too. I think that is wonderful. I am
really a cake eater and have been all of my life. That's why
I have difficulty in keeping my weight down. Soon as I get
up too much I start a rigid diet and then before long I get
hungry for some good cake and up I go again. Will you bake
a cake for me sometime?

Prentiss would even write about his shaving habits, his
tendency to get very sleepy early in the evening, and all the
work he had had done to his teeth.

ഔ ഔ

Ladell continued to worry constantly about their correspondence being discovered, to which Prentiss admonished
her for being "the world's greatest worrier":

What will I do with you if you don't quit worrying about
my secretary and your letters. If I should ever fail to come
home as you say, she will see that your letter is burned. She
is most understanding and has had so much trouble herself
in life she would not willfully cause anyone else any diffi-
culty. So just dismiss that from your sweet little mind, my
dear.

They often wrote of sending each other gifts but apparently never did, primarily out of concern that their episto-
lary relationship would be discovered by his wife or by her
mother:

Sure, you can send me a few tomato seeds. I would love them but don't send too many because I don't have a large spot left for tomatoes. You can send them to the office from D. A. Bonner and I'll receive them, dear, with much affection and will see that they are planted at once.

She promised to bake him a chocolate cake some day (but never got the opportunity). Baking was a big deal among the Allen women. In the 1890s, Caddye won many blue ribbons at the Southeast Arkansas Fair for her baking (I have wondered whether it might have helped that her husband was the President of the Fair Association). Ladell was always trying out her own baked goods, as well as new recipes of all kinds on her bridge club, whom she called her "guinea pigs."

On a rainy winter afternoon, Rebecca walked into the back room, which was the original kitchen, and had a momentary and eerie vision of women in long skirts and high, laced-up shoes bent over a low wooden table, rolling out dough. The vision disappeared quickly, but lingering in the air was the scent of fresh-baked bread.

∞ ∞

When the weather warmed up, Prentiss loved to tell fish stories:

Well, I got home in pieces after a trip that will go down in my memory book. We had one grand time up in Lake of the Woods and caught so many fish we got tired of pulling them in, and that is no fish story either. I got a big musky on my line and played with him for nearly half an hour and got him up to the boat and looked him over carefully,

and when I reached for the pistol to shoot him I got a little
slack in my line and off he went. It was heart breaking, but
some of the other guys caught some. You know those Musky
fish are bad hombres and you have to either hit them over
the head with an oar or shoot them. They have teeth like a
shark and are just as mean. We camped on an island one
night in a cabin and the rain came in torrents and we got
wet through and through, but there was some snake oil in
the cabin so we kept the reptiles away. It's too long a story
to try and tell you in a letter so I'll have to wait till I see you
I guess.

When Ladell's ex-husband, Boyd, died on June 1 in Los
Angeles, she felt a need to explain the arrival of a telegram
for her while she was visiting Prentiss' sister, Genevieve, a
telegram that had evoked an obvious emotional response
from Ladell and led to a sudden end to the visit. Ladell had
remained close to her former in-laws, and she and Boyd still
corresponded. Boyd still told her in letters that he loved her.
Ladell felt she had deceived Prentiss by not being open about
still being in touch with her ex-husband. Prentiss was unconcerned and took the occasion to wax philosophical:

It was sweet of you to explain the telegram that Genevieve
mentioned but it would have been perfectly alright if you
had not. I am not an inquisitive person into other people's
affairs and I can appreciate that everyone has some secrets.
I am sure that the message must have been a great shock
to you because those things have an effect on one and espe-
cially when you have been close to someone, as in your case.

Life has its problems both from a standpoint of happiness and sorrow and we can't hide from them. Even happiness is not easy to attain or to keep, and sorrow of course comes to all of us in various forms. I sometimes feel that regardless of what one does in this life sorrow comes in due time. That I think is the H— we have on earth and we all have our share.

In mid-June, they shared great excitement when Ladell announced to Prentiss that she planned to meet him in Chicago, where he was travelling to on business in just a few days:

You know you caught me flat footed today. Anyway I was happy to hear you are coming to Chicago and I surely will be there to see you. We'll pick ourselves out a place and enjoy the evenings.
Don't change your mind now, sweet.

But something came up and Ladell couldn't make it. Caddye might not have been well (she had broken her hip the year before), or Ladell's explanation for a sudden trip to Chicago had perhaps raised her mother's and Lonnie's suspicions. They might have interrogated her, given her what Ladell called "the acid test." Or Ladell's mother and sister might have invited themselves to go to Chicago, too.

Prentiss was rather peevish about the change in plans:

I'm used to disappointments. I had tentatively made some plans to make your trip enjoyable while here. I have this beautiful suite 2405 & 6 overlooking the Lake. And I got some tickets to a show. Oh well it was not to be.

You certainly had built me up in a big desire to see you in Chicago and I made plans that I thought were going to be to your liking. But bingo—no Dell.

Ladell wasted no time in planning to make up the disappointment to him and to herself and quickly got to work contriving a trip to Minnesota under the guise of travelling part of the way with a friend, Mary, to see Mary's aged mother in Stillwater.

I often think of the very distinct EVP captured in the dining room: "I just lied." Was it a reference to her contrived trip to Minnesota? Or a reference to another time when Ladell felt compelled to lie? Prentiss, of course, was delighted at the new plans:

Your letter came today saying you were now planning on coming up in July. That is more wonderful than the Chicago trip because this one is ahead of us and the other one is gone, so now I will start thinking about seeing you up here. I better be careful about building up too much enthusiasm since something might happen again but I hope it won't.

Ladell explained about Mary and the plan to visit Mary's mother. Whatever she had to do to get to Minnesota was fine with Prentiss, as long as he would get to see her:

I don't know just how you are going to get away from your
hostess but maybe you can sneak out three or four times a
week???

Before she had even embarked on the trip, Ladell was
anticipating the sorrow of having to say goodbye to the man
she had already said good-bye to, with difficulty, in February
1913 and in March 1948. Prentiss was more focused on the
good times yet to be had:

Yes, I hate that thought of seeing someone and then having
to say good-bye. It's awful some times and I dread it, but we
had better look forward to our many pleasures, and maybe
the thoughts of saying good bye won't be so ever present in
our minds. You have given me a lot of happiness too and I
have really looked forward to your letters, honey. You have
been so sweet to write promptly and never have I been dis-
appointed when hound dogging the mail when I thought I
would have a letter. What a woman—so different and con-
siderate and sweet too.

While their correspondence was an important part of
his life, it was absolutely the center of hers. She had tried air
mail, which cost five cents, in an attempt to communicate
with him more swiftly, but he told her the letters arrived no
quicker, to stick with simple First Class postage and to save
her two cents.

Over the next couple of weeks they discussed details of
the impending visit. Prentiss was very much focused on their
privacy and comfort:

Your suggestion about a cottage on a lake sounds mighty good and I am sure that could be worked out in great shape if you would like. Perhaps better than some lake nearby it would be nice if we could run up the North shore (Lake Superior) and really get cold. It is always cold up there with a breeze off the lake and what a relief from hot weather.

Prentiss assured her that he could be gone from home without rousing suspicion and boasted of his independence:

I believe you are the world's champion worrier. Surely I can get away from my home when I have something to do and I surely do have something to do when you are here—I hope. No, I am not and would not live a life of having to account for my time and explain my whereabouts every time I went away. I have been going and coming too long to make myself over—but on the other hand I have had nothing to cover up either, but honey, no one like you has been around, which could explain it.

He was not, however, prepared to throw all caution to the wind:

Better tell me about Mary or rather better tell me how to act around her because I don't know what she knows about me and perhaps it would be best that you tell me what you told her so I can act accordingly. I surely don't want her to get a dislike for me at the start because I might be paying too much attention to you. She might get an idea that I was a wolf or something and of course I am—what do you think?

Just one other thing, honey. Those people you are to visit in Stillwater—tell me who they are because they might know someone that knows someone etc., and I want to be sure that no troubles arrive through being simple minded when it can be avoided so easily if proper plans are made in advance etc. We know a number of people in Stillwater is the reason I ask and I want to be sure you are not visiting people we know—it might be a good precaution to be on the safe side. Now please don't get frightened because I merely want to know about Mary and the host and hostess so I don't find myself running into the few couples H and I know. Doesn't that sound reasonable?

Later, after their time together, he would refer to himself as a "fox" and therefore too clever to get caught. A fox who was a wolf.

Wolf, indeed, and the wolf would not be disappointed.

THE HAPPIEST DAYS

From 2007 to 2010, Rebecca and I had a Halloween tour guide, Shane, who claimed he was "caressed" by Ladell. He insisted it was a true story and told it to everyone, even an MTV producer who was casting for a reality TV show. Shane insisted that Ladell was very "feisty." Sometimes, in recalling the encounter, he used the word "molested," but we cautioned him against exaggeration. Women found this young man very handsome and possessing an air of daring and danger, and they often flirted with him ... until he informed them he was gay. He claimed his contact with Ladell occurred in the master bedroom when he was alone there setting up a CD player on which he would play EVPs for tour guests.

He meant no disrespect or criticism of Ladell. In fact, Rebecca and I insist that all tour guides and paranormal investigators speak respectfully to and of the spirits in the house. Shane merely theorized that, although Ladell was raised to be a "lady" in the late Victorian and Edwardian traditions of the American South, she possessed the desires of a healthy, romantic woman. I think he was probably right.

Clearly, the appeal of Boyd Bonner to Ladell seemed to be his good looks and his "bad boy" personality. He did, after all, operate a pool hall. He was not merely a young man who loitered in one. A pool hall was the kind of establishment many upright citizens of the early twentieth century considered as immoral as bars and as barely more reputable than brothels. During an EVP session in the dining room in February 2010, paranormal investigators asked what Boyd Bonner was like, and an older woman (Ladell's mother, we assume) replied, "Bad man. Drunk every Christmas."

In the 1920s, after the pool-hall business didn't work out for him, Boyd worked as a roughneck in the oil fields around Ft. Worth, Texas, and he and Ladell were renters in a neighborhood where they were surrounded by other roughnecks and their wives or girlfriends. It was undoubtedly an environment and a lifestyle very different from the refined elegance, opulence, and sense of decorum Ladell had grown up in.

She wrote to Prentiss that Boyd's uncle suggested on at least one occasion that she and Boyd have an open marriage to accommodate their individual needs.

Ladell, like lots of people of her time (and ours too), lived a contradiction. She was ferociously concerned about protecting her "reputation," but she was also ferociously determined to love and to be loved. Another way to put this is that she was not just one person but at least two. It's appropriate in the context of this idea that she was known by different variations of her name and was inconsistent herself in the way she spelled her own name: "Ladell," "La Dell," "LaDell,"

"Ladelle," and "Dell." She was determined to fulfill her needs, even if her pursuit of romantic and sexual love violated the morals and mores of her society. Secrets, therefore, were a necessity.

Her life-long friend Frances Roddy Willa remarked that Prentiss sounded better than the "previous others," certainly better than old "Hugh" and "The Mystery Man." Ladell had dated an elderly man for a while, but she had also had the relationship with the prisoner-of-war-camp guard during World War II, who was significantly younger than she was. In regard to Ladell's affair with Prentiss, Frances cautioned her, and reminded her of the fragile nature of her heart and how men were. Ladell had had a lot of heartache, but because of their similar backgrounds and social positions, Prentiss did seem "suitable"—except for that little problem of him having a wife. He was a gentleman, and if he was part "wolf," even part "bad boy" like Boyd, he had class.

In her letters, Ladell would describe the reckless time with Prentiss in the summer of 1948 as the "happiest days of my life." He would too.

☙ ❧

There is a gap in the letters from mid-July to mid-August, representing the time during which Ladell was traveling, first to Greensburg, Indiana, to visit former in-laws who were grieving the death of Boyd Bonner and who always remained fond of his first wife, and then on to Minnesota to meet up with Prentiss and subsequently with her old friend Mary and to spend time visiting Mary's mother, Jene Masterman, in Stillwater.

Ladell arrived in Minnesota on July 28. Except for the time she spent at Jene Masterman's home, she and Prentiss toured Minnesota and Wisconsin in his "big car." She and Prentiss parted at the train station in Milwaukee on August 16, by which time Prentiss was reduced to a quivering, lovesick birthday boy:

My Darling:
I never knew a birthday could begin so happily and end in tragedy. Mine did. I feel like the man who was sentenced to hang and I surely must look like one condemned. How horrible love can be at times—tonight I feel so lonely & forsaken.

Your telegram just came and I was happy to know you are safely on your train. Hope you got a roomette. I felt you would wire me and I love you for it. You are so thoughtful, my darling.

I am going to bed early tonight. In fact I'm ready now and it's not eight yet. I waited until 7 PM and had only some soup and came up here. I could not "eat."

These last five days will live in my memory always as the happiest ones in my entire life.

I love you. Don't ever forget I'm thinking of you always.
P

They were together for most of two and a half weeks, but there was something special about those last five days, and Prentiss was already exhibiting the signs of withdrawal from a potent drug.

He was a huge sports fan, especially of football and baseball. Contributing to his sadness on August 16 was probably the death that day of baseball legend Babe Ruth, who was not even as old as Prentiss—a reminder to Prentiss of life's brevity and uncertainty.

In the weeks and months following their time together, the lovers recalled in their correspondence many details of those two and a half weeks, trying to keep that period vivid in their minds—and making it easy for me to piece together and imagine the events.

∽◦ ◦∾

As the train pulled into the Le Sueur, Minnesota, depot, Ladell's heart fluttered like a trapped bird, like the birds that occasionally got into the house through a chimney or through an open window in the attic. A servant would chase the bird all over the house with a broom. Ladell couldn't stand to watch after a while for fear that, instead of helping the bird find freedom, the servant would slap it dead.

On the platform, Prentiss was there with his gorgeous, luminous smile, wearing a light-weight summer suit and straw hat, shoes polished to a high gloss, his salt-and-pepper hair freshly clipped, his strong jaw smooth and with no sign of a five o'clock shadow although it was past five o'clock.

He rushed up to her as she stepped off the train and grabbed her bag from her and probably said something like, "Dell! My God, it's good to see you. I kept thinking you wouldn't show. I kept seeing myself standing here throughout the night, watching the trains come and go and no Dell. Bingo. No Dell. And then I'd tuck my tail between my legs and stagger home. But you're here. This doesn't seem real.

Are you real?" During the course of his greeting his face reddened and became sweaty. Ladell stared at him. She swallowed. She croaked, "I'm here. I'm real."

"Oh thank God!" And he dropped her suitcase and embraced her. After a second's hesitation, she hugged him back and maybe managed to say something like, "This is better than a letter."

Then they separated and stared at each other, both awkward in the reality of a meeting they had been planning since mid-April.

Prentiss flashed his smile again, took in the sight of her. She fidgeted in her green dress, maybe a Christian Dior to impress him. "Your dress...you look...ravishing."

She stuttered out something like, "Oh, well...well, I hardly think...the dress is...new. I'm hardly new...but my dress is." She giggled nervously. "I'm not making sense."

"No. I mean, yes. Yes, you are. I like the dress. It..." He waved his hands around, seemingly helpless to articulate what exactly it was he liked. Finally, because he could think of nothing more precious than money, he would have said something like, "You look wrapped in a hundred-dollar bill." Then he quickly picked up her bag and said, "I bet you need dinner."

∽◦ ◦∾

She described to him her impressions of the flat green fields of Indiana and Illinois and of the wind and the sky-scrapers of Chicago. She didn't want to talk about her ex-in-laws and said in response to his query about them, "Oh, they're getting along. I felt obligated, you know, to go there, but now I think I'll stay out of Indiana for a while."

Seated at a small table in a crowded restaurant, the nicest Prentiss knew of in the small town of Le Sueur, they struggled at first to keep the conversation going, although Ladell usually had no problem making small talk. Prentiss mentioned that Le Sueur had been the original home of the founder of the Mayo Clinic. They glanced around at other diners. Petite Ladell commented on how big everyone seemed, the women and men all tall and blond and big-boned, the men particularly broad with their padded suitcoat shoulders. "Swedes," Prentiss said. "They're all over the place up here."

She didn't say it, but Ladell thought that she and Prentiss fit right in, looked like any other couple—any *married* couple.

Above all else, she was terrified. She wondered what in the world she was doing. Where would this lead? What kind of woman had she become? For God's sake, Prentiss *was* married. Just not to her.

He said he was avoiding "heavy meals" and ordered a small salad, which he put no dressing on, and a bowl of soup. She ordered the same. He didn't even touch the crackers that came with the soup. She reached for the crackers, but she noticed her hand shaking and pulled it back.

She watched his hands on the table. They were suntanned from his afternoons on the golf course, dark against the white tablecloth, his nails meticulously trimmed. His hands were large, strong looking, his fingers long, fiddling with match books and the silverware.

A small band, an ensemble—piano, bass fiddle, tenor saxophone, trumpet, drums—appeared on a little bandstand, and they played "Almost Like Being in Love," popular since the previous summer. Later, they would do "Some Sunday Morning," a song that Prentiss loved.

Ladell's urge was probably to lay her small white hands over his and to say, *Don't be nervous. Everything is going to be fine.* But she couldn't subdue her own nervousness, and she ordered a bourbon. It made her feel a little less terrified, so she ordered another. Then another. Her head began to feel light.

A month later, Prentiss wrote,

Bless your heart, I can certainly understand why you might have wanted to celebrate a little at Le Sueur because of fear or something, but anyway, I did not mind, and I guess I was under a strain myself, honey, and were I not a confirmed teetotaler I am sure I would have beaten you to that bourbon.

For now, in that restaurant, he talked about the oil business. He loved it. He knew all about it and was good at it. If the Republicans could win the White House that November, his life would be even better. Had to get rid of those darn Democrats and their love of regulations and hatred of big business.

Her vision blurred. Her hearing came and went. She found herself slumping in her chair. She caught only words and phrases. *Stock shares. Drill. Shell. Texaco. Sun. Alaska. Texas. Tanker trucks. Tanker ships. Trains. Arabs. Two thousand feet. Deep ...*

The band played "My Funny Valentine," the piano player gently tapping the keys, the bass player lightly plucking his strings, the saxophone player rocking forward and back, his eyes closed, his face red, the sweet notes soaring through the room and sending a tingle up Ladell's spine. She almost cried.

She hoped she wouldn't throw up, at least not until she could get to the ladies' room.

When Prentiss asked whether she was ready to go, she nodded and stood up, but she sat back down immediately—plop. She apologized profusely, was mortified. He helped her up. She apologized again, murmured that she was very sleepy. He might have said, "I need to get you to bed." And she might have smiled at the thought.

Outside, it was dark and surprisingly cool for July. Wind blew coolly through his big car. Her eyelids were heavy as they alternately passed through stretches of darkness and pools of light. The sidewalks were empty. She maybe dozed for a moment, suddenly finding herself on the swing on the porch of her house; leaves of the tulip trees hung luminously like street lights; she shivered from a cool breeze, and some night bird screeched like a car horn.

Then she found herself standing outside a motel room, and he was saying he would see her in the morning. They'd have breakfast and then he's show her some of "big old Minnesota."

She felt her head bobbing up and down, up and down.

"Are you all right? ... Dell?"

"Yes?"

"Are you all right?"

"Yes." It seems she might have fallen against the door of her room and slid down to the stoop. "I'm fine, I'm fine."

He helped her up, helped her unlock the door, helped her to the bed. "I'm so sorry," she said. "You're so sweet."

"Get a good night's rest. I think you just got some bad bourbon."

And he pulled the door shut and was gone. *A gentleman,* she likely thought, just before she threw up and passed out.

In September, she would write:

Some of the memories of my visit are hideous. How I would hate to think the few remaining years of my life would be spent like the phase of my stay in Le Sueur.

ఆ ⌇ ⌇

The next morning she probably woke up with her heartbeat throbbing in her head. She found herself in a strange, dark room. Maybe for a few seconds she wondered if this was what death was like.

Then just as she remembered she was in Minnesota, a sudden rap at the door startled her. Another rap, and she lifted herself off the bed and felt her way across the room, the linoleum floor cool to her feet. She opened the door a crack to blinding and painful daylight.

"Dell. It's me. Prentiss. Remember me?" Then Prentiss may have joked, "Typical of a woman not to remember the man's name the morning after."

She would have gasped, touched her dress. He *was* a wolf!

"I'm just joking, Dell. I'm sorry. Bad joke. Please forgive me. I was being crude, wasn't I?"

"No, no, I'm the one who should apologize." The door was still open only a crack. "I'm the one who has behaved so badly. You must think I'm a total ... a total lush."

He assured her that he had nothing against people having a few drinks, but in his letters that autumn he did occasionally express concern:

Back home you won't be drinking much I am sure and I am really glad because it does not help you, darling. I really want you to be a sweet pretty little old lady when you get old and you can and will, I know.

❧ ❧

He bought her a newspaper so that she could check her horoscope.

After lots of coffee, which Ladell liked with much cream and sugar, and a light breakfast, they headed out in Prentiss' car. He drove slowly, enjoying the scenery and telling her the names of the lakes and parks and various attractions of "big old Minnesota" as they traveled north. The windows were down, and the day-time air was surprisingly cool on her face. This was not like Arkansas, where getting hit with a breeze in summer was like being smacked in the face with a hot, wet towel. Her head cleared more and more. Her jangled nerves quieted.

In downtown Minneapolis, he drove her past his office building, pointing at a window near the top, but of course they could not stop anywhere in the city. She felt fluttery again as they drove the downtown streets. She slumped low in the seat, ready to duck under the dashboard at his command ("Oh, God, there's the mail boy!" or "Oh, God, there's Helene's best friend!" or "Oh, God, there's my secretary!"), but he never gave such a command.

She was curious about his secretary and would not have minded a glimpse of her. After all, the secretary had worked for him for seventeen years and handled his mail. She maybe knew more about him than anyone else on earth. She probably ordered anniversary and holiday flowers for his wife for him. She would have transferred to him calls from young women who asked in a familiar way to speak with Mr. Savage—if there had been any young women. Despite his constant reassurances that his secretary could be trusted, Ladell worried about the woman, was uncertain (based on her own experiences and actions) that any woman could be completely trusted, and she wanted to see what this woman looked like. She knew what sometimes happened between men and their secretaries.

Ladell was a bit calmer after they left the city and traveled narrow blacktops hugged by dense walls of trees, but she was still nervous and concerned.

Prentiss was terribly nervous, he would admit in his letters. As he drove, he talked about his work, golf, fishing, hunting, baseball, football. Words were like a fisherman's line and hook—silence would allow the fish to escape.

She liked it that he talked of manly interests and pursuits although she didn't always understand and sometimes didn't hear all he was saying as her mind strayed. She watched his well-manicured hands on the steering wheel and studied his brown forearms now that he was wearing a golf shirt instead of a suit. Muscles rippled when he turned his wrists.

They read historical markers and hiked through parks. He pointed out birds to her and talked about their nest building and their mating habits. She was impressed. Men usually didn't know about birds. They just shot them. He shot them, too, certain kinds, and with great enthusiasm, but he also knew about cardinals, blue jays, swallows, egrets, owls, woodpeckers, robins, and hummingbirds. Their appearances and disappearances, he said, told him when to get out his golf clubs and when to put them away, but he also appreciated their beauty and their songs. "Wait," he would say when they spotted a song bird. "Maybe he'll sing for us." And they stood frozen and so quiet that she could perhaps hear her own breathing and could perhaps imagine she heard her own heart beating—or maybe it was his. If the bird performed, Prentiss said, "Wasn't that nice?" She marveled at his smile, his sensitivity, his intelligence, his good looks. It was no wonder he had more friends and money than he could count.

Along the rural roads, she noticed several billboards that simply said "EAT" in huge bold letters. At first she thought it was an acronym. When she realized that the signs indicated a restaurant ahead, she said that it was like a command to eat, wasn't it? Or if one thought about it, it could be a command to ... and she made a joke that made them both laugh and blush. In September, Prentiss wrote:

I'm sure the food you served to your club was good to "EAT." Every time I see one of those signs I think of you,

darling—it really was funny and I never thought anything
about them before.

ᕤ ᕥ

The vacation was going well, and his absence from home
seemed not an issue at all. Shortly after Ladell returned to
Arkansas, Prentiss wrote that his wife never suspected a
thing. He even said he thought God had been looking out
for them, helping them keep their secret. God seemed to
approve:

> *The Lord has been on our side all the way and I am sure*
> *he will keep his hand on my shoulder as he has done for*
> *several weeks now (meaning that you have come into my*
> *life, darling).*

Prentiss did sense some disapproval, however, on the part
of Ladell's friend Mary:

> *I have not heard from Mary and am glad. I was hoping she*
> *would not call ... I am sure you are right in not telling her*
> *about anything you did or any place you went. Friends are*
> *wonderful but it is not well sometimes to tell them every-*
> *thing and as a matter of fact I tell mine very little ... But I*
> *must run out and take her mother some candy or something*
> *before very long. She was so sweet.*

Ladell had not been entirely honest with Mary about her
motives for the trip or her plans once she arrived in Minnesota. Indeed, there was no correspondence with Mary about

Prentiss or at least no correspondence from Mary to Ladell about him. Mary's mother, Jene Masterman, though, simply thought Ladell was sweet and charming and was impressed with her male friend and hoped to see both of them again:

Of course we are going to see each other again—the door is always open, & I might add the attraction [Prentiss] not far away. Shall be glad to see him any time, for LaDell I enjoyed you every minute you were here. Only wish it had been longer.

But Ladell couldn't stay longer at Mrs. Masterman's. She and Prentiss had plans. They drove north to the Northernaire Lodge on Manitoulin Island, Ontario, Canada. Prentiss would complain that the coffee cost "four dollars a cup" and was no better than dime-a-cup coffee, but otherwise he would have no complaints.

At sunset, they took after-dinner walks along the banks of the lake, the sun spreading its warm colors across the water.

He had not been much of a wolf, after all. It appears that he waited for signals from Ladell, who could be bold when she got far away from home. In fact, she worried that he would not like her if he saw her at home because she would have to be different:

Then we can meet—& see if you still feel as you did in Wisconsin & Minnesota. You know one can change their opinion of a person—after all I am different on my <u>home</u> grounds.

Prentiss wrote back saying he hoped to find her no different and couldn't fathom what she meant, unless it was that she drank less when she was at home. He really didn't seem to understand that she was warning him that she would have to be more reserved near home, would feel less free.

At Northernaire, no longer even in her own country, Ladell was far from Arkansas, far from her mother and sister and the town gossips and notions of how a Southern belle should conduct herself. She had not drunk since that first night and was proud of herself. She was happy. Prentiss was wonderful. She wanted him for her own, and she knew one way to make acquiring him a possibility.

The evening air was so cool in this beautiful place, the trees so tall. The lodge was on a peninsula in a sheltered bay. The lake rippled gold and pink with the late sun. The word *"Fore!"* may have drifted on the breeze from the distant golf course.

Prentiss mentioned that, if he were on vacation with anyone else, he'd probably have brought his golf clubs. That other person would have seen little of him.

Ladell would have told him he should have brought his clubs. She never wanted to deprive him of his interests or pleasures but only wanted to learn how she might share them with him. "You could have taught me," she would have said.

"If you'd really like to learn, I will. I'll teach you. Yes. *Certain* people never wanted to learn."

"The same certain people who don't like to travel with you?"

He nodded. "Yes, the same certain people. You, on the other hand, are about the best little traveling companion I've ever had."

It was perhaps in a moment like this that she said something like, "If I'm such a good travelling companion, then why haven't you tried to kiss me?"

ᥫᦅ ᦅᥫ

They devoured each other the way they began to devour offerings of the resort restaurants. Stacks of pancakes, eggs over easy, links of sausage, and slices of buttered toast. Steaks and lobsters and French onion soup, baked potatoes smothered in sour cream. Veal, frog legs, catfish, salmon, flounder, shrimp, duck, pheasant. For dessert, wedges of cheese cake, cherry pie, apple pie, pecan pie, lemon pie, chocolate cake, chocolate mousse, or chocolate ice-cream. And they drank gallons of coffee:

I came home weighing about 7 pounds over my normal weight. I did not realize I had eaten so much but there are lots of things a person forgets when his sole interest is centered on the person he is with.

They apologized to each other for gaining weight.

But there was no need to apologize—they loved each other. Neither found fault in the other. They made love and fell deeper in love. Prentiss later wrote:

You are so right when you said nothing will ever excel the Wisconsin trip. I guess that will go down in my memory when other things in life are forgotten. It was the most beautiful, eventful and satisfying trip I ever had and nothing could ever replace that, I am sure.

⁂

Ladell later asked whether she had been in Appleton, Wisconsin, and Prentiss said yes. In fact, Appleton was where she and Prentiss almost got caught together by her friend Mary and Mary's husband:

> *Yes, you were in Appleton ... Would have been a nice how-do-you-do had we met them on that Sunday, eh? ... I still get a kick out of you being scared at Wisconsin.*

Prentiss stopped talking so much about the oil business and golf and hunting and baseball. He mostly talked now of his miserable marriage and how he didn't want to be miserable any more. Instead, he wanted to be married to Dell:

> *I know now more than ever that you and I should work out the details we talked over. I shall do my part soon, I hope.*

Much too soon, it was August 16, Prentiss' fifty-sixth birthday, and Ladell had a train to catch.

MAPPING THE PAST
AND THE FUTURE

During a summer 2010 investigation, a particularly well-equipped team of paranormal researchers used a "ghost box" to make contact with the spirits. This was no inexpensive jerry-rigged Radio Shack transistor radio or a free app for an iPhone. The five-thousand-dollar ghost box allowed for something tantamount to a "live" EVP session. One function of the device was the generation of ambient sound that spirits could manipulate. The investigators explained that spirits needed something to work with, some kind of energy with which they could manifest themselves audibly. The ghost box also had amplifiers and a digital readout screen. The result was that we could hear the EVPs as they were spoken, not just when recordings were played back, and the words spoken by spirits appeared on the readout screen.

The investigators first used the device in the library where, when switched on, it immediately and repeatedly said, "Sad. Death."

Then, for a while, the investigators asked questions to which there were no responses. The room was dark and felt calm. And it was silent, except when an investigator asked a question, after which we would all wait.

The ghost box did not speak.

The EMF devices did not blink.

The temperature in the room did not change.

Then about fifteen or twenty minutes into the session, I spoke up, as I usually do when investigators start asking questions based on Allen family myths or historical inaccuracies—I'm a stickler for facts and small details. Somebody said something about Ladell being married at the time of her affair with Prentiss, so I started explaining to the investigators about Ladell's divorce in 1927, her subsequently managing a hotel in Memphis, and the strange census record showing female roommates named Ladell and Clide and male roommates named Ladell and Clide, even the spellings identical, living in the same hotel. The K2/EMF meters flashed wildly as I talked. The room felt cold and charged with energy.

My belief in the ghost box became solid when it said "Ant." Everyone in the room said, "Aunt? Whose aunt?" Then the team member sitting on the floor next to the device said, "No. There's an ant crawling on the floor." It was clear to all of us that a spirit was in the room and had observed the tiny ant near the curious box.

Upstairs in the master bedroom, the team again conducted a session using EMF meters, digital audio and video

The Library

recorders, and the ghost box. Among many other words—and while the EMF flashed and flashed—the ghost box said, "summer" at least twice and "Mary" three or four times. Repeatedly, the ghost box said, "Driving. Driving. Driving."

ᴄᴂ ᴆᴧ

In his letter of August 19, Prentiss enclosed folded gas-station maps on which he marked in red pencil the roads they had traveled and the towns where they had stopped:

Miss Allen:
Just drove home and found no one in the office so it gives me an opportunity to fix the maps of Minn. and Wisconsin and send them along so you will know just where you were, my dear.

He indicated that, in addition to Le Sueur, Stillwater, Minneapolis, St. Paul, Appleton, and Northernaire, they had been to Mankato, Oshkosh, Eau Claire, and Land O'Lakes.

During the entire vacation, Ladell had had trouble getting her bearings. It all seemed so unreal, so wonderfully dreamlike.

Although she, of course, still had to keep the relationship a secret from most people, Ladell was eager to share the news of her love affair with three confidants. She was bursting to tell people she felt she could trust about having found a long-searched-for happiness.

She first wrote to her friend Frances Roddy Willa, a woman who had grown up in Monticello with Ladell. Frances, a former school teacher, had married into money and had a summer home in Nova Scotia, where Ladell had visited her in June of 1944, and another home in Newton Center, Massachusetts, just outside of Boston. Frances replied quickly and excitedly, but with a word of caution and with a reference to Ladell's fragile heart. Underscoring the closeness of these two friends, Frances' writing possessed many of the same stylistic quirks that Ladell exhibited in her own writing, especially when attempting to express emotion:

Dear Dell:

Phew-w-w!!! I'm glad I was seated when reading your letter (I'm still grasping my chair) for certainly yours was "blow-me-down" news! I have read your letter several times, and each time I have chuckled, chuckled, chuckled in enjoyment of the surprise, and I can't help comparing my reactions to some of the previous ones—There was Hugh—for in-

stance—*a good old sort, but with such abysmal ignorance that I couldn't feel happy about him. Then the Mystery Man! I was in a near panic about him (tho you never knew just to what extent). In peacetime I don't like hustle-hustle affairs individuals. There are too many nefarious schemes and subversive affairs in our uncertain world of today. I was truly relieved when he petered out. This one would seem to have the best chance of happiness for you, which is what counts with me. I have so very much wanted you to find someone suited to you unquestionably. I shall be all agog until I know that all the wheels run smoothly, until everything is worked out. Do keep me informed.*

I can just imagine what a lift you could give Prentiss after years of the stodgy personality of the wife you described. I wonder if I should recognize him after about 30 yrs since I've seen him. Has he changed any?

Goodness gracious! I wish we were together so we could talk, talk, talk, instead of writing. Where does Prentiss live now? And about his divorce—will she consent to give him one and get it (there seems to be a feeling it's the chivalrous thing to let the wife get it, tho I notice less so now than formerly). If not, can he get one? Can he find grounds? Sometimes these virtuous wives make it difficult. However, incompatibility is sufficient in some states, and he can go wherever necessary. Judging from your letter, plans are to proceed at once, so he can go South after it is settled in the fall.

Dell, dear, you know your heart, so play your cards accordingly—carefully!! 'Cause men are unpredictable.

*Write again soon and keep me up to date. Much love to
you.*

Frances

*P.S. Of course you may depend on it: "Mum is the
word!"*

Marie Wootten, who was teaching Ladell about Christian
Science, replied with a rather positive response of her own to
learning of Ladell's love affair:

My Dear:

*Your letter just received and I am so grateful you have had
such a glorious trip. I know you have come home with renewed hope. Know God is on the field directing your every
thought and action.*

And Prentiss' sister Genevieve didn't need any explicit
explanations. She had easily figured out what was going on:

Dearest Dell:

*Was disappointed you couldn't return via Helena so we
could have a chit-chat—and then to find that you were in
Memphis visiting your niece, and I was there, too—anyway, thanks for your note. Sorry you couldn't give me the
high-lights of your trip, but I read between the lines that
you had a most enjoyable one … Had a letter from Prentiss a
few days ago. Contents not at all surprising.*

Ladell wrote to her three friends with certainty that Prentiss would soon divorce, that her future was mapped out

with confidence. The road was clear and straight. He would divorce, quickly, and retire from his position at Texaco, and then he would move to Arkansas under the guise of wanting to be near family (his sister in Helena and his elderly mother right in Monticello). She and Prentiss would start seeing each other openly, making a show of being old friends just becoming re-acquainted. Then they would allow the public to perceive them as courting. Out of respect for their families and decent society, they would wait awhile to marry, but "not too long" because they both felt they had already wasted thirty-five years. They might or might not stay in Arkansas. Ladell loved her home state, thought it was the best place in the world, but Prentiss said the hot summers would be hard on him. He was no longer used to the heat and the awful mosquitoes and would prefer the cooler summers of the Colorado mountains or Washington state.

Maybe the small details weren't entirely worked out, but Prentiss seemed determined to move forward with their plans, as quickly as possible, and was adamant in professing his love:

> I have thought of you so very much, darling, and I could never think of any plan working out except the one we discussed and I am holding onto that one thought that it must be and will be.
>
> The very worst thing in the world happened to me in Milwaukee when you left—I felt that I had lost everything dear to me, and I cannot describe the feeling of loneliness that came over me when I walked away from that train and knew you were gone. I hope I never never never have to experience

anything like that again in my life. They say time heals all wounds and I guess it does to some extent, but I still wish you were here, darling, so I could see you. You are so sweet and I just love the cute little way you have of saying things—it is all so individual—no one else can say them as you do.

I am so in hopes that before many weeks go by that I will be located at the club and that maybe something will bring a quick release from this bondage.

He even suggested in one letter that everything might be resolved within two weeks if "H" cooperated. It would be a simple matter of filing papers, and after a wait of one week, he would be free, in accordance with Minnesota divorce laws.

The night he returned home from his vacation with Ladell (or "business trip" as some people believed), he began "negotiations" with his wife. He and Helene talked into the early hours of the next morning, and Prentiss was a weary wreck the next day, but surprisingly, his wife had listened calmly and thoughtfully and seemed agreeable to a divorce, to ending a marriage from which neither "party" derived much personal benefit or pleasure.

∽◌ ◌∾

For about three weeks, Ladell was incredibly happy and allowed herself to be optimistic about her and Prentiss' future. Her feeling that she had recaptured her youth, along with finally finding true love, was reinforced by Prentiss, who kept reminding her of her ageless beauty and addressing her as "Miss Allen," figuratively erasing thirty-five years of a disappointing adulthood.

A word that the paranormal investigators' ghost box said several times on that night in the summer of 2010 was "jewel." Ladell was fond of jewels, certainly. How fond she was of jewels was underscored by the fact that in her letters she addressed Prentiss as "Pearl."

What she pushed away from her mind were the possibilities that Prentiss' wife might decide she wanted everything, might not cooperate whatsoever, and that Prentiss was caught up in a decades-old pattern of living, a pattern of habits he enjoyed, habits predicated on his love of his job, money, and sports.

And Ladell had control over nothing. Everything was up to Prentiss. He was in the driver's seat, and although she at first had faith in his steering that big sedan into the future, the way she had trusted his literal driving on their tour of Minnesota and Wisconsin, her role was merely to wait, and she had already waited so long, and the distance between them was great. She couldn't reach over and touch his knee and easily remind him of the pleasures that awaited once they arrived at their destination.

She could only put her faith in the stars and hope that the optimistic horoscopes were accurate. Prentiss was a Leo, and she sent him a horoscope about "Leo the Lion Hearted," a horoscope that shored up her confidence in Prentiss' ability to successfully follow through with all the plans they had made. He too enjoyed the bright predictions of the horoscopes and told her to keep sending them.

But by mid-September, haunted by a past of romantic failures, Ladell would be working at reclaiming her title as the "world's greatest worrier." That clear, straight road that led toward a bright future was veering off into a very dark place.

ᴄᴏ *Chapter 17* ᴏᴠ

ROUGH GOING NO WOMAN
WOULD ENJOY

As the weeks passed following the bliss of August, Prentiss wrote vaguely of the difficulty of obtaining a "settlement" he felt would be fair to him and his wife both.

In mid-September, Ladell was reaching out anxiously to Marie Wootten for reassurance that God still wanted her to have this happiness she had found relatively late in life. Marie responded:

> *Yes, I shall continue to stay with you and, honey, don't allow yourself to get discouraged. That is the tool of the devil and remember—the vacation worked out, didn't it? And all this other good has come out of that—so—be grateful and "rejoice evermore!"*

Surely annoying, if not downright troubling, to Ladell was Prentiss' writing of enjoying the company of his grown step-daughter, Jerry. They had dinners together, just the two of them, and even went to shows together:

> *Tonight I am going over to the Lyceum with Jerry and see Bert Lahr and Rochelle Hudson in "Burlesque."*

Then he sounded uncharacteristically moralistic in praising the lifestyle of comedian Bert Lahr while at the same time implying that it was difficult to remain righteous in both the entertainment business and the oil business:

> *I always did like Bert Lahr. He is one of the few comedians that is white and still married to his first wife after 25 years or more. That speaks rather high for him, don't you think—especially after being in show business. Show business I guess is like being in the oil business. I wonder which is the toughest.*

And he wrote fondly of his mother-in-law:

> *H. and Jerry are both still up north, and her mother is with me and I love her. Last night late when I came in she was so sweet and was sitting up waiting for me. She is a little put out that H. went up north and she told me she would not think unkindly of me if she saw me with some girl. Now that is being broad minded. It all came about in our discussions about things in general. She is so understanding and sweet and I always have loved her and always will, I am sure.*

Ladell wondered whether Prentiss could really be so naïve and stupid. Clearly, his mother-in-law was trying to get information out of him about an infidelity so that Helene would have a powerful case when the divorce went to court. Amazed and disturbed by his *naïveté*, Ladell tried to restrain herself in opening Prentiss' eyes to reality:

> *Am sure Mrs mother was insincere when she said she could not censure you if she saw you with another woman.*

And Ladell looked for reassurance that Prentiss The Wolf was not actually on the prowl in her and his wife's absences:

> *Doubtless you feel about that like I did when Boyd's uncle suggested it—Boyd go his way—& I go mine , but not me —that way of life is only temporary happiness. I know my honey is not a Philanderer as that would not be the happiness you want & so deserve.*

Prentiss assured her she was correct. That "way of life" was not for him. He had confidence, he said, in their fidelity to each other:

> *I just would not believe that you would bestray [sic] my confidence. Even if I saw it, I would question my eyesight. There is no reason why either you or I should be unfaithful in any way and I know my conscience would not let me bestray [sic] a trust and I would not think of doing so under any circumstances.*

But he went on so long about the issue that it makes me wonder whether he actually did have some concerns—concerns about *her*:

> *I just won't allow myself to even think there might be someone else seeing you in Monticello, Little Rock, or Memphis.*

An additional frustration for Ladell was that he was not clever enough to know when to ignore her directives. He had asked about phoning her long distance so that he could hear her "sweet voice," but she told him it would be too risky. Her mother might answer, and a person couldn't trust telephone operators, especially the local ones. Nonetheless, she actually hoped he would call:

> *I had quite a thrill for the moment, Sunday night, when the phone rang for Long Distance. My heart was in my mouth. I thought you were calling. While I did tell you I hardly thought it wise at this time, I was hoping you~~knew~~ would disregard that. After all it would not be so very unusual for a L. D. call to come over this phone but I <u>wanted</u> to be the one to answer & hear the operator say <u>Minnesota</u> calling Mrs. L.A.B. Maybe someday you <u>can</u>—may—or will— <u>which</u> do I say?*

They continued to discuss the possibility of talking on the phone, especially when he was going to be staying at hotels and, at least for his part, would be safe from eavesdroppers, but it was never convenient or safe for Ladell. The last time she ever heard his voice was on August 16. After that, there were only letters.

Although he wrote nearly daily throughout the last two weeks of August and throughout September, he continued to write hurried, one-draft letters, whereas Ladell labored over multiple drafts and made lists of possible subjects (much like the lists she wrote on the door-frame molding inside the closet of the master bedroom):

L Distance

F yard

Friday 13—weeds

Horoscope

Va ???

athletic club—Letter

L.R. 83319 $30.00—train case

Gwyn?

L.D. call—

Ashes

Corinne

EAT

Grip covers

clothes pressed

gained weight

Radio Programs

Repaired

couples bridge

Fog

Patterns of silver

L.D. call?

X-mas ribbons

L.R.

Oct.

Letters arrived morn

Prentiss started to write about the difficulty of sitting down with "H" for further negotiations. They were both gone so much—he on business trips, Helene on trips north to shop for antiques or to seek relief from her allergy attacks—and every time he had a chance to talk with her, he had to start at the beginning, and she was not so agreeable as she had been during the first discussion of divorce. She wondered why now, after twenty years, he suddenly wanted his freedom. She also had an "inflated" sense, he said, of her contributions to the marriage and was looking to get most of the stocks and bonds and cash reserves and real-estate. Prentiss even flirted with the idea of travelling to Genevieve's home in Arkansas so that he could hide some stock certificates. He regretted but defended his putting his wife's name on financial documents many years before as something he just didn't think about at the time. After all, he never imagined he would be trying to get a quick divorce someday to be with the true love of his life. In any case, he was determined not to be "taken." He and Ladell would want to maintain a certain lifestyle, and Ladell was already worrying that a future with her own true love might require a vow of poverty. Prentiss told her they would not be so poor she wouldn't have a ring, and he tried to re-assure her further:

> *Don't worry about us, honey. We'll get along and I am sure we won't have to live on black coffee and doughnuts. All I*

*want is to be fair in my treatment and in turn I hope to be
treated fairly, and if this can be worked out on that basis, I
will be happy with whatever I have to do to settle. I would
not want to leave and feel that I have been unfair in my settlement because that would hurt me and I don't want to feel
that way in future years. I want to leave with a feeling in
my heart that I have been fair and honorable. I hope it can
be worked out on that basis. If it can be, we'll be in good
shape, darling.*

She admired his desire to be "fair and honorable," but
the bottom line for her was that he was making no progress.
He didn't even move to the athletic club as he had planned
to. He explained that until he and his wife agreed on the
terms of the divorce it would be best for him to "stay out
at the house." Moving to the club would incense "H," and
she threatened to make a stink if he did. He wanted to avoid
the kind of scandal the newspapers "would love to get hold
of," but "H" wouldn't mind a scandal one bit. It was his great
mistake, he said, to have married a "Yankee woman."

Also annoying to Ladell was the way he wrote more and
more about his sadness that the golf season would soon end.
Who cared about golf! Although they both listened to the
radio broadcasts of the baseball World Series in which Bob
Feller was pitching for the Cleveland Indians against the Boston Braves, it was a short-lived mutual interest, and his letters
became dominated by his passion for University of Minnesota Gopher football games, which he attended without fail
every Saturday the Gophers played at home. He was hoping
they'd make it to the Rose Bowl and was abjectly depressed

when their chances were destroyed by a defeat at the hands of Michigan. Ladell could not have cared less.

He wrote extensively about his plans to take several hunting trips in October and November. He always took hunting trips in the fall to South Dakota, North Dakota, and Montana. He spoke of the hunting trips as if they were absolute necessities. He had a new gun and was eager to try it out. He told her he'd be thinking of her as he blew those birds out of the sky.

What about *their* plans? Ladell wondered. Their plans for a life together.

Surely unaware of the symbolism that she might have read into the statement, he wrote:

> *It's a strange thing but I have lost all interest in my pretty little roses, and they are wilted and to be dying from neglect.*

She started to wonder whether his preoccupation with hunting might become an issue for them as a couple in the future. Always considerate and generally willing to adapt to please others, Ladell suggested she would go with him on future hunting trips, but his response was not encouraging:

> *Yes, it would be nice if you could go on these hunts, but honey, we don't allow women. I don't believe any woman could keep going through corn fields and share the hardships that one must face. It is rough going and I am sure no woman would enjoy it.*

He did suggest that he could maybe throw caution to the wind and make a trip to risky Memphis, where they could meet up at a hotel for "an enjoyable time."

By the middle of October, Ladell's frustration boiled over, and she accused Prentiss of not really loving her after he made the suggestion that they meet in Memphis, a suggestion unaccompanied by any promise that he would be divorced anytime soon. Such a suggestion implied that he didn't really love her but only thought of her as a "fast" woman he could use for pleasure. She wrote that she didn't want to see him until everything had been "settled in a court of law." Then on second thought she admitted she did want to see him, but the meeting would be highly proper, so proper that even her mother would approve. It would be only in the lobby of a hotel and only for half an hour, insisted Lady Ladell.

Prentiss' own frustration was evident in his response and even provoked a rare instance of sarcasm:

> *Coming to Memphis and sitting in the lobby for a half hour would be so exciting I am afraid I could not stand it, honey. What a suggestion! You are sweet to think of such a rare happening, darling, and if I did not know you as I do, I would think that gal surely does not love me.*

Following this outburst, Prentiss calmed down and tried to re-assure her that he loved her as much as ever, that his feelings had not changed in any way whatsoever:

I am so unhappy that I wrote you that I wanted to see you in Memphis or someplace because I can see now that you are thinking I don't love you and I want to tell you that I love you more than I ever did, sweetheart. I have no such thoughts as you imagined and there is no change in my feelings toward you and I don't see how there could be, darling, because I think of you almost constantly and with love.

Ladell was too much in love and had too much emotionally invested in seeing their vision of the future become reality to give up. She would not allow their relationship to unravel now.

To reassure herself or to convince herself that their plans were still solid, she went to the attic, retrieved his letters from their hiding place under the floor, and re-read them all. With a pencil, she marked the envelopes of letters she considered particularly important. She wrote "1st discussion" on the envelope of the letter in which he mentioned his first discussion of divorce with his wife. On other envelopes, she wrote "2nd discussion" and "3rd discussion." On two, she wrote "Jerry" and "J." On another, she wrote "1st wk December." On a couple she simply marked an X.

On the letters themselves, she wrote "X" next to certain paragraphs, such as the following:

I am so hopeful that by October or November something definite will have taken place, and if so, then I will come down.

And she made simple vertical lines next to other passages and squiggly lines next to some, generally sentences in which he mentioned his efforts to divorce his wife and his plans to move to the club and subsequently to come South. She also marked passages about their possibly meeting in Memphis and about their being together at the holidays.

In the end, after reading through approximately fifty letters she had received from him up to that time, she concluded that she had been silly, that it was obvious he still loved her and loved her as much as ever. She could look forward to Christmas. Surely by then, all would be resolved. She apologized profusely, to which a relieved Prentiss happily responded:

> *It must have been a source of much satisfaction to you to have gone over a bunch of letters and find that no change has taken place. Well, why should there be, even if you were all agog the other day and thought so many things were wrong and how I had changed and everything. You are just a woman, darling, and I guess women have those queer feelings occasionally.*

She even finally responded to a request he had been making for several weeks: that she send a photo of herself. She, however, sent a very old photo, one taken with her sister Lonnie Lee, and she insisted that he return it immediately:

> *I should be mean and say I will return it when you send me a recent one I can keep but I won't do that because you said to return it and I am enclosing it as you suggest but*

there is a great temptation to keep it. It looks so much like you even if it is a few years old. May I congratulate you on not having on one of those stove pipe hats like Lonnie Lee. I hate those things and I am sure that if that is ever the style again and I find you with one, I will discover some way to lose it for you. I never did like those hats and I guess I never will. No, honey, I would never have known Lonnie Lee. She is much fatter, but you honey—you look as sweet and cute as ever.

As the dense foliage of Arkansas turned autumn colors and Halloween decorations—ghosts and witches and skeletons—appeared, things seemed back on track. A little delay, but the plans had not changed.

Not yet.

WRONG NUMBER

Well-equipped to the tune of a quarter of a million dollars' worth of devices, they said, the group of paranormal investigators who came to the house in the summer of 2010 wanted to evoke the atmosphere of Christmas 1948 in the master bedroom. The lead investigator donned a white lab coat and stethoscope to play the role of Dr. Johnnie Price, who was Ladell's attending physician between December 26 and January 2. Dr. Price was the one who recorded on her death certificate the words "suicide" and "mercury cyanide poisoning," as well as her time of death: eight pm.

The investigators placed various Allen House artifacts in the center of the room on the floor, including two of Ladell's liquor bottles, the photo of Ladell as an infant, a couple of Prentiss' letters, and the china plate from which she ate her last meal.

They said their chief means of evoking Christmas 1948 would be to play holiday music from that time. With the lights out and the K2/EMF meters, thermal meters, video cameras, digital audio recorders, and ghost box turned on, the lead investigator switched on his iPad and clicked on Bing Crosby's classic "White Christmas."

Crosby's mellow baritone filled the room in which Ladell had deliberately consumed mercury cyanide as her mother hosted her annual Christmas party downstairs.

Before coming upstairs, Ladell had socialized with the guests for a while, smiling as usual but a bit distracted as she kept looking around, her eyes flitting here and there as if she was looking for a particular guest she was anxious to locate among the crowd. Guests complimented her red dress. Prentiss had told her that red was her color, that she should always let herself be noticed, let herself be the center of attention. Most people, he had said, had never seen anyone like her, because she was a queen.

Late in the evening, after guests stopped arriving and a few began to leave, Ladell ascended the grand staircase with hors d'ouvres on a china plate. Ladell ate the hors d'ouvres, which she may very well have made herself. Had she tried out a new recipe for the party that she already knew would likely be her last, unless a certain person made a surprise appearance and saved her from herself? The hors d'ouvres helped to mask the taste of the mercury cyanide tablets, as did some punch.

More than sixty-one years later, "White Christmas" did not play long before the ghost box spoke: "Wrong number." In the 1940s, tunes played on the radio were regularly referred to as "numbers." Then as the lead investigator placed his iPad on the bed, the ghost box—as if someone wanted to underscore for all of us in the room that we had company—said, "Sheet." And if that wasn't clear enough, the spirit in the room with us said, "White." Yes, the sheet was white.

⊷ ⊶

In early November 1948, Prentiss' letters no longer came with regularity or frequently:

I have tried all this week to get down to writing you but I have had too many visitors and I just could not get a minute to myself.

He wrote vaguely of being overwhelmed by out-of-town guests and feeling sick and being burdened with "personal problems." He was angry over Helene insisting that he give up more than he was willing to in a divorce. The following is about as specific as he ever got:

If it will help any I have talked with my lawyer but the big talking has to be with someone else as you know and that will come at the right time and I can't rush that. If I appear too anxious it will be more difficult so I will let it take shape in due time and it will be much better all around. Some people can't be rushed and you know who I mean when I say that.

He was also terribly upset about the Democrat Harry Truman winning the presidential election. He didn't understand why the Democrats hated big business, he wrote. The way he saw it they were "giving the country away" with all their "give-away programs." He inserted a brief apology in one letter, noting that Ladell was a Democrat and he didn't mean to insult her. Then he went right on with his political rant. All kinds of plans that Texaco Oil had made in the hopeful anticipation of the Republicans taking power were now in the "discard box," and he was going to have to come up with all kinds of new ideas. Texaco Oil's plans? Ladell wondered. What about their plans, his and hers?

She wanted to know exactly what the time line was now, what exactly his attorney had said, what exactly Helene was saying. Ladell asked him questions he never answered:

You asked me several questions and I will get around to answering them as soon as I have time ...

You mentioned in your letter that you were waiting for an answer to the questions in your letter on Saturday. I thought I had answered all of your questions, but if I did not, tell me what it is I did not answer, and I will try and do so.

He no longer signed his letters "P" but "X," presumably a symbol for a kiss, but also perhaps a subconscious expression of a desire to efface himself.

She gave in to his desire to see her in Memphis, even if it was risky and dangerously close to home and had all the appearance of being improper. She didn't care so much anymore about things appearing proper or improper. She needed to see him, to know that he still loved her. They made tentative plans to meet in Memphis in late November or in December, and in any case he looked forward, he said, to being in Arkansas during the holidays and would definitely see her. The plan to meet in Memphis perked him up, and

"Prentiss the Wolf" wrote that he was even willing to sit in a hotel lobby with her but that somebody would have to tie his hands down because he knew he wouldn't be able to keep his hands off her. He went go to say:

You are quite a nice little tonic, darling. Even if only in the lobby—which I know would not be for long.

But the Saturday following Thanksgiving, there was a decidedly negative shift in a tone and mood that had already been mostly gloomy. Something had happened. His wife was making things harder than ever and seemed more suspicious than ever. She had put a good scare into him and had dropped on him a mountain of guilt:

The way things are now I do not believe I had best try and go to Monticello during the holidays because this would complicate things more than they are and I do not wish for that. I would love to come down there but you will understand.

Understand? Ladell did not understand, not at all. She repeated questions that he continued not to answer. All he could tell her was that he still cared for her but that things were incredibly complicated and difficult. He rambled on vaguely about how he knew nothing anymore for certain:

My letters of late perhaps have not sounded very pleasant but then I have been having my problems and I don't know the answer. It is so easy for someone to say just go ahead and do so and so, but when it comes to doing it, one finds it much more difficult and especially if there are some other things to get settled that you just can't seem to settle. It is hard for me to write you just what I mean but I am sure you understand that when one pulls one way and the other another, solutions are hard to find. Am going home and to bed as I feel achy and maybe when I again attempt a letter I can do better. You will agree I am sure I could not do worse.

While she tried to re-assure him with horoscopes, he had clearly come to doubt their predictions:

I enjoyed the horoscope you sent—it makes good reading even if all the things said are not exactly so.

In an attempt to distract herself, Ladell went to Memphis to visit her nephews, Robert and Lewis Jones, and her beloved niece, Martha Anne Jones, whom she had visited in August on her way back from her vacation with Prentiss. Martha had then come to Monticello in September. Surely, Martha noted a change in Aunt Dell's mood and must have wondered where her aunt's energy and quick wit had gone. Aunt Dell looked worried, was starting to show her age.

Ladell enjoyed seeing her nephews and niece, but seeing them did little to lift the depression descending as the most important romantic relationship of her life slipped away.

Winter was coming. In fact, it seemed to have come early. Prentiss wrote:

I guess you are freezing to death.

There had already been an ice storm that had covered much of Arkansas, and had made the roads very hazardous. The world was terrible and frightening. Hunters were shooting each other in Minnesota, Prentiss said. People were sliding off mountains in Arkansas.

And Christmas was coming. She would have all kinds of social obligations throughout the holiday season—when all she wanted to do was be alone and cry.

Then it would be 1949, and in March she would turn fifty-five. Good lord, she thought, she was getting old. A quick downhill slide to sixty. Maybe fifty-four would be a good age at which to end it all. Papa was fifty-four when he died.

ひ෧ ௫ல

Eerily, from the beginning, signs of death were everywhere in the Prentiss-Ladell relationship.

The day of their reunion after a separation of thirty-five years, the day at the race track, March 10, 1948, was the same day that Jazz Age icon and romantic Zelda Fitzgerald, wife of *Great Gatsby* author F. Scott Fitzgerald, died in a fire at the mental hospital where she was a patient.

In his second letter, at the end of March, Prentiss mourned the recent death of a mutual acquaintance and alluded to the deaths of Ladell's son and younger sister. Then in another early letter, there was the evocation of the suicidal evangelist Aimee Semple McPherson.

In his letter of May 15, Prentiss wrote:

I thought of you as we were flying alongside the Canadian Rockies.

Weirdly, he described them as "like great big tomb stones." In that same letter, he referred to hearing about the suicide of a woman in Monticello who "was found in a pond," and he added,

> *Too bad those things have to happen to people, but poor health and unhappiness cause many things.*

In his August 19 letter, Prentiss enclosed an obituary for a "Prentiss Savage":

> *A friend of mine in Denver sent me the enclosed clipping and said this is the way my name would look in the obituary column some day. How morbid but I thought it was so unusual I wanted you to look at it, dear.*

Ladell shunned the morbidity of the clipping and threw it away. She was probably superstitious about it, especially since she constantly feared Prentiss' dying in a plane crash or on some remote road.

In other August letters, Prentiss wrote of a woman dying of leukemia and of the death of "an old friend and mentor."

In a letter of her own in mid-September Ladell alluded to her own mortality:

> *How I would hate to think the few remaining years of my life would be spent like the phase of my stay in Le Sueur.*

About the same time, Prentiss, too, alluded to her mortality:

Don't wear yourself to pieces cause I want you to live a long time.

Also in September, Prentiss commented:

You will worry yourself into your grave.

On November 8, Prentiss wrote:

Did you ever see a ghost walking? I am one.

Indeed, within a month, the flesh-and-blood Prentiss—as represented by his letters—would vanish. He would become a mere ghost, a figurative one whose parting words and subsequent silence would haunt Ladell for the few final, miserable days of her mortal life.

∽ ∾

At the end of November—in what turned out to be his next-to-last letter—Prentiss again complained of being ill, and he somewhat regretted not getting to do any deer hunting. He made a final "wolf" reference that was creepy and perhaps illuminating when we consider the injection of the deer analogy and the fact that he had always linked wolves to himself:

Anyway, I don't like deer that well. I mean those four legged animals not cute little ones like you, honey ... The hunters are not getting many deer this year but instead it seems the timber wolves are killing many deer. You know Minnesota is noted for big bad wolves, and they are as large as police dogs and much more vicious.

On the morning of December 2, Prentiss was up early, preparing to leave on his long-planned business trip to New York City, and he wrote a rushed and morose letter, his last to Ladell:

My dear:

Today I am off for the big city. Am leaving at nine this morning and will be gone until the 11th. I don't know just how I will find time to do much writing but will try and drop you a note while I am there.

Was glad you could go to Memphis but am sorry I could not have been there too for a visit. My letters are not so hot but between getting ready to go east and other personal problems I just can't seem to write like I should like to do. It surely seems to me that when trouble walks in everything else seems to walk out. I am sorry it is this way but, dear, it can't be helped. I never realized that the plans I had in mind would be so terrifically difficult to carry out, but that is the way it looks. Maybe the ray of sunshine will come thru the clouds in time, and life will take on another view-point. It is not all financial problems but there are others and that is what makes it difficult, as you can understand I am sure.

Have been going to the dentist for the past few days and I am glad that is over. What they do to your nerves is awful. I can't stand to listen to those drills humming.

Must run as I am sure somebody will be coming into the office soon but wanted to get this note off to you while I had the chance.

Take good care of yourself, dear. Love.
X

               ඟ ඞ

In the falling temperatures and growing gloom of early and mid-December, Ladell found no delight in the holiday decorations going up on the town square or in her own house. She turned to Genevieve to help her understand what was happening, but Genevieve was not hearing from Prentiss either:

Well, honey, I am also "up a tree" now—I have heard nothing more in regard to the plans for Christmas. Thought if he could come—he would let me know. I imagine H is putting up a pretty big fight—I think he meant "other <u>problems</u>" besides "financial"—I don't blame you for feeling as you do about the whole thing and think you are right about the letter writing. As Arthur [her husband] so often says in reference to business deals "just let 'em sweat awhile." I am far from being a Dorothy Dix [1861–1951, popular advice columnist]—only wish I knew human nature as she does— maybe I could advise you on the course to follow. Of course you know I'd never mention you writing me as you have. I love you for the confidence you have placed in me. Maybe by now you have received a letter or letters that are a little clearer and not quite so business-like in tone.

Let's hope & pray that everything will work out for the best—come what may for all concerned. Well my dear I do hope you will have a happy Christmas and that the new year will bring to you joy and happiness -

   Fondest love—

   as ever—

   Genevieve

Ladell expressed her depression to all three of her confidants, but no one was equipped to comfort her. Frances wrote that she had been concerned all along and wasn't terribly surprised by Prentiss' failure to extricate himself from his marriage:

You gave me so little <u>news</u> about you and Prentiss in your last letter, saying only that things would have to be postponed. Didn't you know I would be seething to know <u>what</u> and <u>why</u>? Is it, as I feared, that "mama" would not let him go without putting up a battle to keep him, and if so, is her ammunition too much to cope with now? That being the case, what will be yours and P's grand strategy? Or has anything else entered the picture in the way of uncertainty? Please let me know because I am so interested and have your happiness and welfare close to my heart.

Genevieve offered the opinion that Helene was probably taking the advice of an attorney and insisting on a separation rather than a divorce and was doing everything in her power to assure she lost none of her financial security. Feeling helpless, Genevieve told Ladell she hoped they could still be friends even if things did not work out for Ladell with Prentiss.

Perhaps least helpful—and possibly even harmful—was Ladell's spiritual advisor, Marie Wootten, whose responses were grounded in the cryptic teachings of the Christian Science Church:

> *I denied your last letter as an expression of reality. There is one God—there is one man. God is the only Cause and Creator and man cannot be outside of omnipresence! Yes, you do know what Christian Science is!! In Miscellaneous Writings I found this on page 208: "Mortals have only to submit to the law of God, come into sympathy with it, and to let His will be done. This unbroken motion of the law of divine Love gives, to the weary and heavy-laden, rest." Now rest your case with him, dear one. Stop fighting Him! "Let there be light" is the demand. Read that article in Miscellaneous writings which begins on page 208 [of* Science and Health, *the guidebook authored by Mary Baker Eddy for her Christian Scientist followers, first published in 1875]. Then examine your motives in this situation. If we are trying to run away from a situation or to outline what is best for us—these concepts must be purified. "Behold, I shall send an angel before thee to keep thee in the way and to bring thee into the place which I have prepared for thee." (Ex.23:20).*

෧෧ ෨෨

The daughter of the couple who bought the Allen House from the widow of Karl Leidinger, Jr., in 1986 told Rebecca that Mrs. Leidinger spoke of Ladell to her parents, saying that it was known among members of the Allen family that

Ladell often called out the name of her son in the middle of the night, presumably in her sleep. For that reason, many in the family accepted the theory that Ladell had committed suicide out of grief over her son's death. Of course, a weakness of the theory was the fact that Allen Bonner had been dead nearly five years by Christmas 1948, and other than the claims of family members that Ladell spoke his name in the night, Ladell appeared to have dealt with her grief over Allen's death fairly well.

She never mentioned Allen in her letters to Prentiss or to her confidants. At the time of her suicide, her grief was clearly focused on the failure of her and Prentiss' relationship. What is likely, however, was that Ladell was aware of Allen's presence in the house. Allen haunted her, perhaps not so much figuratively or psychologically, but literally.

If, for over half a century, the various residents of the house have been aware of Allen Bonner's ghost, it makes sense that Allen was present in the years between his own death and his mother's. The third-story turret room that had been Allen's "special place" became Ladell's in those years. It was the place where she hid and re-read Prentiss' letters and drank rum and wine in secret, and perhaps where she felt close to her deceased son. It was perhaps Allen's presence that aroused Ladell's interest in Christian Science, a faith that claimed death was an illusion.

To Ladell's thinking, was the presence of her son's spirit evidence that there was something to the idea of death being a mere illusion?

∽ ∾

I have no doubt that Ladell wanted her story to be known—
at least eventually. After all, it is not as though she died suddenly or unexpectedly. She planned her suicide and could have
destroyed the letters. In fact, Genevieve explicitly asked that the
letters she wrote be destroyed, as well as letters that Prentiss
had written to Genevieve and that she had forwarded to Ladell:

*Had a letter from Prentiss a few days ago and will enclose
same—just destroy.*

Ladell destroyed none of them.

She had kept the letters in their original envelopes and
then placed batches of them into larger envelopes, as though
to better preserve them. The house had four fireplaces. It
was December, so the servants kept the fires going all the
time. If she had wanted to reduce the letters to ashes, it
would have been easy. Instead, she left them in their hiding
place, and when no one was left alive who could potentially
be embarrassed by the life she had led (that is, after the death
of her niece Martha Anne Jones in August 2009), Ladell led
someone to them. Maybe she chose me because I'm a writer.

The following letter was the last among the eighty-one
pertaining to Ladell's affair with Prentiss. It's from Marie
Wootten, to whom Ladell had been sending checks in
exchange for spiritual guidance and reassurance. Now Ladell
had obviously confessed to a loss of faith and to having suicidal thoughts:

Dear One:

Now, you just stop that self-pity, young lady! We cannot get anywhere in the world if you stop to indulge that attitude of thinking. "Rise in the strength of the Spirit to resist all that is unlike good." All good is yours right now but you have to first prove yourself—who you are (the son of God)—in order to claim it. And if you will look on page 242 you will see why we can't indulge the quality just mentioned and get anywhere. Don't you see that with one breath you are claiming your heritage and then, with the next, you are declaring that you are mortal and denied all these things! You know a house divided against itself cannot stand.

Now—come on Gal—we are standing! We are seeing the salvation of the Lord in liberation! Come on—stand and sing praises to God! In joy and peace will your freedom be realized! It is here—claim it!

In these remonstrations, Marie Wootten illuminated a contradiction within Ladell. While Ladell acknowledged her own worth and her right to happiness, she could not bear or deflect the pain of her disappointment, the pain inflicted by another. Ladell was, indeed, a house divided.

The final words of this final letter are particularly eerie:

In joy and peace will your freedom be realized. It is here— claim it!

Surely, Ladell was thinking she would free herself of her emotional agony and find peace if she killed herself, and it appears that Marie Wootten may have, unwittingly, pushed Ladell further toward suicide rather than discouraging the idea.

Marie assured Ladell that "rest" and "peace" lay with God, but first Ladell must prove herself, prove who she was—" the son of God." The son of God? How did Ladell interpret Marie's call to action and the statement that she denied herself all that was good by declaring herself "mortal"? Did "joy and peace" lie in the sacrifice of her body and thereby her assertion of her immortality? In other words, would killing herself allow her to know that pain and death were what Marie claimed they were? Illusions?

Marie's Christian Science took a metaphysical view of Christianity in which pain, disease, sin, and death were all mere illusions because they were not of God. But did Ladell really believe that a toothache was an illusion? That the pain in her heart at being neglected by a man who promised never to neglect her was an illusion? It's no wonder we have a very distinct (what paranormal investigators call a category A) EVP from Ladell saying, "I'm confused."

And she felt she had no control. She was on a very tall ladder that was falling backwards.

Although no one can know what exactly Ladell was thinking when she took the mercury cyanide, it is clear that she was distraught over Prentiss' lack of progress in freeing himself from his marriage and over his silence since his letter of December 2. He had not told Ladell, in so many words, that their relationship was over, had never said, "I'm sorry but I'll never see you again." However, he had clearly indicated that any plans they had made were now on hold. He had had to toss out all kinds of plans for Texaco Oil because he'd had no control over that "damn Harry Truman" winning the presidential election, and now he had to toss out his and Ladell's plans because he had no control over the complications of his marriage. Or at least that was his claim.

He and Ladell would have to wait, and he didn't know for how long—maybe forever. He was no longer assuring her that he would keep his promises. He was still signing his letters "love" and expressing a desire to see her, but instead of suggesting a place and a time when they could meet, he only expressed regret at being unable to meet. He was hesitant to even mail her a Christmas gift, an overnight bag if he could find one he knew for certain she would like; he would probably just send her some cash, he wrote. Yes, that might be best: send her some cash. For Christmas. How romantic.

Then nothing. No more letters. He was in New York City and surely busy, but was a quick note really impossible? Even after he was supposed to be back in Minneapolis ... silence. For more than a month he had been signing his letters "X." A kiss or a cancelling out, a figurative effacing of himself? Now he had literally effaced himself.

Certainly, she had built up so much anticipation of being with him during the holidays that the disappointment was too painful for her to bear. But if she had made up her mind that life was intolerable, was she aware that mercury cyanide was more likely to lead to a long painful death rather than a quick escape? Was she aware that many people actually recovered from the ingestion of the poison? Could her taking the poison have been not a wholly sincere desire to die but a cry for help, a desperate attempt to get Prentiss to come to her?

౾ ౿

Since March, Ladell had gotten up early in the morning, and even before the servants had coffee ready, she left the house to go downtown to pick up her lover's letters from post-office box number 144. Then she walked to the drugstore in the next block. She would sit with a cup of coffee, read the letters, and draft responses in pencil. For several months, she was frightened, excited, and happy. After all the failed relationships—Boyd, Hugh, "The Mystery Man," and others—she had finally found love.

But winter had come and a cold silence had descended.

Then on Christmas Eve, a Friday, she made the trip to the post office. But again, there was no letter. Perhaps she was thinking about something Prentiss had said back in August:

I guess this old world would be an unbearable place in which to live if we did not have ... someone.

Or she might have been thinking of something she wrote to him in October:

We are lucky to have each other to live for.

Or perhaps she likely felt anger mingled with her pain and thought that what she had in mind now would serve as suitable punishment for the man who had said:

I don't want to experience that feeling of you leaving me alone again. I felt sheer regret.

Yes, that was exactly what she had in mind—she would leave him alone. She hoped he suffered terrifically ... Or no, maybe not. It was difficult for her to wish ill upon another. And she loved him. If she could just end her own suffering, maybe ... maybe that would be enough.

She then walked to the drug store, but without a letter to read, she did not sit to drink a cup of coffee. Instead, she stood at the pharmacy counter and made a purchase that would long haunt the guilt-stricken pharmacist: a bottle of mercury-cyanide tablets, triangular in shape, and to be applied topically to sores.

‹ი *Chapter 19* ჲ

MEANT TO BE?

In February 2010, during an EVP session, a group of para-normal investigators asked, "Do you know who Prentiss is?" There was a response, and it was from a female, but it didn't sound like the voice we usually associated with Ladell. It sounded like the older woman we assumed was Caddye. She said ambiguously, "He was a big man." This could have been a reference to his physical stature or to his success as a businessman or to his importance in the life of Ladell.

I have often tried to imagine what it must have been like for him when he heard of Ladell's suicide attempt and her death a week later. Genevieve probably called him long distance the day after Christmas as soon as she heard that Ladell was in the hospital. She probably heard the news from her daughter Virginia, Ladell's close friend. It was Sunday, and the phone call would have come to Prentiss' house, and although there was risk in that his wife would be present, it was news he needed to receive right away. The terror and sorrow in Genevieve's voice as soon as he got the phone must have caused his gut to clench like a fist. The news must have surely horrified him as much as anything he saw in France in 1917. All those corpses.

There is, however, no evidence that he visited Ladell in the hospital or attended her funeral. Prentiss was a practical man. I believe he saw no reason to put his reputation at further risk, especially with the loss of Ladell, who was his only motive for putting it at risk in the first place. And being a practical man, he never divorced his wife. She and his niece Virginia were his only survivors listed in his obituary when he died in April 1978 in Stillwater, Minnesota, at the age of eighty-five.

How often over those thirty years after Ladell took her own life did he think of her? Did he often try to imagine how different the final decades of his life might have been if she had not killed herself and he had eventually been able to extricate himself from his marriage? He was a practical man, so maybe he pushed such speculation away as pointless, but this was also the man who believed, at least at one time, that his and Ladell's love affair was meant to be:

> *Your letters have become such an important cog in my wheel of life that it seems strange that I did not have them before I came to Arkansas last March. And incidentally it was exactly six months ago today that I left for Arkansas and on that trip found that sweet little darling in Monticello. I certainly had no idea that it would turn out as it has. Had I missed you on the last trip, the chances are I would not have ever seen you again—who knows? Therefore, my darling, I believe it was to be, regardless of what else happened.*

Was his belief in the pre-destination of their love affair undermined by Ladell's suicide? But, again, Prentiss was a practical man and probably found little point in contemplating the question of fate for very long. For him, Ladell's suicide was likely just further confirmation that life was hell, that life consisted primarily of sorrow and pain. Again, no point in thinking a lot about it, though. There was an oil company to run, a trucking business to operate, money to be made, a reputation to preserve, Elks Club meetings to attend, golf games to play, football games to cheer, fish to catch, and birds to shoot. These were the things that made life tolerable.

But he did visit Monticello after Ladell's death. The elderly woman whose husband was Prentiss' nephew said Prentiss visited several times throughout the 1950s. What did he think—what did he feel—when he passed by the house? Or did he avoid passing the Allen House? Did he ever sneak off by himself while in Monticello and visit Ladell's grave in Oakland Cemetery? Did he stand over her block of granite and say, "Why?" or "I'm sorry"?

It appears that Genevieve never told anyone of the affair, not even close family members. And why would she? Nothing good could possibly come from people knowing about her brother and Dell Allen Bonner. It was a secret Genevieve took to her grave in 1965. She had not even told her daughter Virginia. It seemed no one in Monticello knew about the affair because no one really knew why Ladell killed herself. There was just all that speculation: she was sad over the death of her son; she never got over her husband cheating on her; she had never gotten over her soldier lover leaving her; she was an alcoholic ...

Ladell and Prentiss' secret was safe. But he must have wondered about all those letters he wrote to Ladell. He must have worried about them. He must have wondered where they were. He might have assumed or at least hoped that Ladell destroyed them.

Over time, his concern probably diminished, but for a while, he surely wondered and worried. Those letters could do great harm to his reputation. The newspapers would be full of the scandal! His wife could use the letters against him in court, no matter that the woman who had stolen his affections was dead.

∽ ∾

About Prentiss, the spirit of Ladell has had no direct comment, but about her life and her choices she has commented quite a bit. The EVPs "I just lied" and "It was justified" are consistent with her attitude and actions. She also has said, "I'm confused" and "It was awful, awful." And, "I should not have done it." Of the dozens of EVPs investigators and Rebecca and I have recorded, there has not been one so far that said "Prentiss." Instead, the voice we assume is Ladell has repeatedly said "Michael" or "Mike." The first "Michael" EVP was one of the most distinct from the first full investigation ever conducted at the house. We do not know who Michael was. Perhaps, he was the "Mystery Man" Frances Roddy Willa referred to. Perhaps he was the soldier who left Ladell at the end of World War II. He could even be the man who was with her in New Orleans in late 1945 and whom Lonnie Lee disapproved of. Men were drawn to Ladell, but the relationships never lasted. Ladell seemed to anticipate Prentiss changing his mind about her. That was the pattern she had grown accustomed to—men falling in and then out of love with her. Maybe her neediness drew men to her but ultimately repelled them.

The startlingly harsh EVP "She killed him"—in reference to a young man killing himself after being rejected by his lover—reflects Ladell's attitude that the lover who withdraws affection is to be held accountable for the actions of the one abandoned.

People often ask Rebecca and me why the ghost of Ladell doesn't say "Prentiss" over and over. My thought is that although she wanted her story told she doesn't want to speak the name of the man whose neglect drove her to desire death over life. She's perhaps like the characters in a short story by Ernest Hemingway entitled "Hills Like White Elephants." The characters are identified only as "the man" and "the girl," and the story is difficult for first-time readers of it, because the characters never speak directly of the subject that is causing tremendous stress in their lives and relationship. The girl is pregnant, and the man is pressuring her to have an abortion, but the girl is not so sure she wants to or can, although she loves him and wants to please him. Neither character ever says any of the emotionally charged words that would make the discussion unbearable. They never say "baby," "pregnancy," "fetus," or "abortion." Perhaps, Ladell cannot bear to speak the name "Prentiss."

ॐ ॐ

Although several people, including some paranormal investigators, wondered whether Ladell would remain in the house after the discovery of her letters, the revealing of her story, she is clearly still with us.

During the February 2010 investigation, Rebecca felt sensations she had never before experienced. An EVP session was being recorded in the dining room, and she felt as though Ladell was trying to get her to speak for her. Rebecca's entire body felt cold, and a heaviness weighed on her chest. Breathing became difficult. Her hands tingled. Her vision blurred. When an investigator asked Ladell which party at the house had been her favorite, Rebecca felt powerfully compelled to blurt out, "Thirteenth birthday!" but she held it in and said nothing. The investigators later revealed that the EVP response they received to the question was "Nineteen seven." Ladell turned thirteen in 1907.

When an investigator asked whether Boyd Bonner was a lush and a womanizer, Rebecca felt Ladell rush out of the room in a huff that reminded Rebecca of a peevish adolescent girl. We would later find out that Caddye responded affirmatively that he was a "bad man."

The intimacy Rebecca experienced with Ladell was so unsettling that she told me about it only several days after the investigation. She said it was something she had needed to think about for a while before attempting to articulate the experience to someone, even to me.

There's the hint of tension between mother and daughter in Ladell's rushing out of the room subsequent to Caddye criticizing Boyd, whom Ladell felt affection for all her life no matter how disastrous their marriage may have been. The mother-daughter tension is suggested in another incident that occurred in the dining room. One day Rebecca and a friend were having lunch at the dining-room table beneath the cherubs and the large chandelier. When Rebecca's friend started talking about how her mother tended to drive her crazy, the chandelier started to flicker a little. Then the friend said she'd have to put up with her mother on Christmas, and a light bulb on the chandelier exploded, detached itself from its socket, and dropped onto the table. Startled, the friend, who knew the story of Ladell's Christmas suicide, said, "Sorry! Sorry! Didn't mean to touch anybody's raw nerve!"

I'm not surprised that Ladell is still with us. After all, the others are here in the house, too. I don't think Ladell stayed simply to oversee the letters, or was "trapped" because she committed suicide. There seems to be some choice involved in all of these spirits being in the Allen House. And why would Ladell want to leave her son, her mother, and her father?

Rebecca and I, as well as various paranormal investigators, believe that Ladell, Caddye, Allen Bonner, and probably Joe Lee Allen himself occupy the house. The man in the big hat Rebecca has seen twice (once in the second-floor hallway and once in the foyer) is probably Joe Lee, a man who was a bit of a dandy and would have worn an ostentatious hat without a second thought. He had a rather flamboyant bearskin coat that he had himself photographed in. The story behind the coat was that he used to keep a live bear chained up behind the Allen Hotel. One day, he got angry at the bear or realized that the bear could be a serious liability if it got loose and ate a guest, so he shot it and had it made into a coat.

Rebecca has also seen a woman she believes is probably Caddye. Looking down the main staircase from the second-floor landing, Rebecca saw the back of the woman as she walked in the foyer toward the front door, the way the man in the big hat had. The woman was small, her shoulders rounded. Her hair was done up in a gray bun on the back of her head. This same woman was perhaps one of the women Rebecca saw rolling out dough in the original kitchen one rainy winter afternoon. And there are all those EVPs that seem to come from Caddye.

The matriarch of the Allen family initially didn't like the investigators who came to the house in February 2010. As they were about to begin their EMF-and-EVP session at the dining-room table, the voice of an older female said, "Leave this house!" I'm not sure what the issue was, but the investigators picked up another EVP at about the same time, the female blurting, "Rebecca!" as if Caddye was upset that Rebecca would let these people into the house. Caddye's displeasure on this occasion might have been carried over from an investigation a few weeks before this one when we had some ghost hunters in the house who were baiting the spirits—until Rebecca and I told them to stop, that we would not allow baiting. I had overheard an investigator in the attic asking Allen Bonner if he was a coward and if he was a "homo." The EVPs from that investigation were few and consisted primarily of "Jerk" and "Go away."

For several minutes, the team of investigators in February 2010 asked questions about Ladell and Allen Bonner and Joe Lee to which they received no audio responses, and the EMF meters sat on the dining-room table inactive. Then an investigator asked whether Caddye was present, but he mispronounced Caddye's name, calling her "Katie." An EMF started blinking wildly and did not stop for at least three minutes.

The Dining Room

While those little colored lights flashed with what seemed ferocity, the lead investigator apologized and professed no disrespect toward anyone in any way. Caddye and some other spirits subsequently accepted the presence of the investigators and, amazingly, answered a wide range of questions.

When Caddye was asked about her favorite kind of music, she answered, "Gospel." As mentioned already, when she was asked what she thought of Ladell's husband, Boyd Bonner, Caddye said, "A bad man," and then, "Drunkard." When asked how her father died, Caddye answered, "It was a runaway horse." In fact, historical records indicate that B. H. McKennon, Caddye's father, was killed by runaway horses in 1875. The voice of Caddye Allen added that her father had been a veteran and buried in Memphis. Although I have been unable to confirm his place of burial, I do know that B. H. McKennon was a Confederate veteran (because he is listed as Allen Bonner's ancestor on the 1933 membership roles of The Children of the Confederacy) and that B. H. McKennon enlisted at Memphis.

In response to a question about the Allens' rental hearse, two male voices seemed to compete with each other to answer, one saying "Was from Jonesboro [a town in Arkansas]," the other saying "Was from Memphis, had oak bed." Then a woman said, "It had horses," and, indeed, the hearse was drawn by horses.

When the spirits were asked who liked playing with the Spencers' Victrola in the front parlor, a woman said, "It wasn't us," and then a male, probably Allen Bonner, said, "Mother."

When the investigators asked what Caddye's sister, Mamie, taught, a woman replied, "Sunday School"—again an historical fact.

Joe Lee Allen seemed to make contact via a provocative EVP in which the voice of a man said, "Grab the cash under the closet." Then a female said, "Papa's nest egg."

I'm hoping it was an interactive rather than a residual EVP, and I only wish they had been more specific about

The Victrola

the location because I haven't found any cash yet and it's an awfully big house.

ↄ๏ ๏ๅ

The spirits, including Ladell, seem to occupy the house for general rather than specific reasons.

The house was Joe Lee's grand monument to his success and prominence, an ostentatious and beautiful display of his wealth, and the place where he could best enjoy the company and affection of his wife and three daughters.

Allen Bonner lived most of his twenty-eight years in the Allen House with his grandmother, climbing with his friends up into their turret clubhouse in the attic. His friends from Monticello High School and subsequently Arkansas A & M College came over, and they all had a good time with "Duke"

Bonner in "the party place of Monticello." The attic was his lofty domain of fantasy and fun. No wonder he chose it as his eternal home.

The Allen mansion was Caddye's home for nearly fifty years. Before the mansion had been built, she had lived in a smaller house on the same site, so in all, she had lived in the same spot for sixty-four years. She was very much a part of the old place and it was very much a part of her. Some things about Caddye's life were the same for an awfully long time. At the time of her death in July 1954, she still had the same phone number she'd had in 1897 when telephone service first became available in Monticello.

In her waning years, was she, like Ladell, perhaps aware of Allen Bonner's presence? Some people believe she was aware of Ladell's. Perhaps she locked up the master-bedroom suite to keep things the same for Ladell. Rebecca and I have all the house's original keys that Caddye used to wear on her waist, and I wonder whether Caddye, the keeper of the keys, may have sometimes unlocked one of those doors to the master-bedroom suite to enter and sit and talk to her sad and confused girl.

In late 2010, as I worked on this book, Caddye apparently wanted to provide some clarity as to why she and the other spirits remain in the house. She gave us this clarity one afternoon while Rebecca was making a movie with the kids in her film school. (The movie was thought up by a seven-year-old film student and was about a little girl whose irate piano teacher chopped off her hands after a particularly poor performance; the little girl became a ghost who haunted future piano students.) When Rebecca started watching and listening to the raw footage of the filming she had done in the front yard, she was startled to find that one of her cameras had picked up a fairly lengthy and distinct EVP. Among the voices of the children in the movie, an adult female voice suddenly injected words that eerily mimicked those of a Louisiana Spirits investigator. During an EVP session in the attic in June 2008, the investigator made the comment, "The spirits in this house are very loving," to which the voice of an older woman responded "They are." The EVP Rebecca recorded in the front yard in late 2010 didn't say "They are," but it said in a voice similar to the investigator's, "The spirits in this house are very loving. The family likes it here."

Then on Christmas day 2010, the tuning knob of an antique radio reappeared after having been lost for more than two years. The kids all swore they never had anything to do with its disappearance, and on Christmas morning, it showed up beneath a little Christmas tree on the desk in my study. Rebecca and I believe Allen Bonner, the prankster, decided it was time to give it back.

That night, on the sixty-second anniversary of Ladell taking mercury cyanide, I fully charged my cell phone before going to bed and then left it on a vanity in the master bedroom. In the morning, the phone—unused since being fully charged—was dead. The battery was completely drained. In previous years, I had not noticed Ladell being particularly active on Christmas night, but I did note that Christmas 2010 fell on a Saturday, as it had in 1948, and I wondered whether that might have mattered to Ladell.

In early 2011, I started to open the upstairs bathroom door one morning, and it seemed somebody gave it a shove, almost as if the person was trying to knock me down. I thought, *One of the kids was pushing it.* I was about to say, "Hey! What the heck!" when I saw that no one was there. A moment later I heard a loud smack and saw that a broom standing against the wall in the hallway had fallen over.

I said nothing about these little events, but in the car, after we dropped the children off at school, Rebecca said she hadn't wanted to say anything in front of the kids but that she had a strong sense of somebody in the house being upset about something that morning. She also told me that, as we were leaving the house, Jacob said to her out of the blue, "Did somebody die?" When she asked him why he asked such a thing, all he said was, "I don't know. Cause it's raining?"

Then I suddenly recalled what day it was: January 25 was the day Allen Bonner's body arrived at the house for his funeral in 1944.

∽ ∾

One of the mysteries that remains for us is the identity of the ghost children. Louisiana Spirits recorded a child singing and a child saying, "Be quiet." A tour guest in 2009 recorded on her cell phone a wonderfully distinct EVP at the top of the servants' staircase. In a lilting voice, a little girl said, "These are the stairs," as if this little ghost girl wanted to be a tour guide.

The paranormal investigators who came in the summer of 2010 apparently got things stirred up because shortly after they left late that night, I walked from the master bath out into the second-floor hall and found Rebecca crouched on the floor with her back against the wall and struggling to breathe. I kneeled beside her and asked what was wrong. I put my hand on her shoulder. She was trembling. For a couple of minutes, she stared straight ahead, at nothing. I looked for signs of physical trauma. Finally, she caught her breath and began to tell me what happened.

She had come up the servants' staircase, turned to her left, and confronted there in the fully lit hallway a small child, probably a girl, but it was hard to be certain. The child wore what appeared to be a white nightgown and had no hands and no feet and no facial features. Its face was a beige blur. Its dark hair surrounded its head like a halo. The sight was so vivid and so startling that it had literally taken Rebecca's breath away and had triggered her gag reflex. She says that as much as she still loves the house she could have done without that particular experience. It was different from the other things she had seen in that it was so close, so vivid, and stayed materialized so long.

Similar to the way Prentiss and Ladell speculated whether their love affair was destined, Rebecca and I have wondered whether, in the grand scheme of things, we were meant all along to become the owners of the Allen House.

The career opportunity for me at the university was unexpected—my application had been a matter of chance, almost a lark. I had actually been offered more money to stay at my old university, but I felt drawn to Monticello, Arkansas, in part by the sense I got of a rich history.

Looking back, Rebecca and I find it eerie that there's such a strong connection between Ladell and the letters and the rental house we first lived in.

It's interesting, too, that Marilyn never considered selling the house until we approached her.

The Second Floor Hall

Rebecca and I certainly faced challenges in purchasing the Allen House, the first and only house we truly fell in love with in our new town. Even after we purchased and moved into Sylvester Hotchkiss' 1902 Victorian and found it to be wonderful, we still felt that the Allen House was meant to be our home. Living in the home of the architect who designed the Allen House seemed a mere preamble to living in the house we were meant to have.

And, finally, things worked out. The Allen House became ours.

We felt early on that the house needed us, but we found that it perhaps needed us in ways we could not have imagined in the beginning, and we could not have imagined the ways we would be changed by the house, the ways it would contribute to our personal growth and our knowledge of life—and death.

Aside from being a bit scary and creepy at times, the Allen House has enriched our lives far beyond our expectations, and I like to think that the spirits we share our home with feel that we've given something to them, as well.

A CHRONOLOGY OF ALLEN HOUSE FACTS

September 20, 1863: Joseph "Joe" Lee Allen was born to Sarah and W. M. Allen. Joe Lee's father died before Joe Lee turned six.

1870: Virginia (Mamie) McKennon was born. The older sister of Caddye McKennon Allen, she never married, dedicating her life to helping raise the Allen children and to teaching the kindergarten class at the First Methodist Church in Monticello, Arkansas.

1870: According to the 1870 census, thirty-nine-year-old Sarah Allen, Joe Lee's mother, was a "farmer." The Allen household consisted of Minnie, 16, Lonnie, 8, and Joseph, 6.

March 12, 1871: Caddye McKennon was born to B. H. McKennon (1840–1875) and Carrie Reeves McKennon (1842–1925). B. H. McKennon was a Confederate veteran, serving with Company 2 K, 38th Tennessee Infantry. He enlisted August 28, 1861, at Memphis, Tennessee, and was paroled May 1, 1865, at Greensboro, North Carolina. He was killed by a runaway team of horses a month before Caddye's fourth birthday.

October 1, 1890: Joe Lee Allen and Caddye McKennon married. Joe Lee owned a livery stable on East Gaines Avenue in Monticello. In later years, he sold automobiles, in addition to horses, mules, buggies, and wagons. He owned the Allen Hotel, a private school, and a horse-drawn rental hearse. He became the first president of the Commercial Loan and Trust Company and served as president of the Southeast Arkansas Fair Association. In 1908, Acting Governor Pindall appointed him treasurer of Drew County.

September 8, 1891: Lonnie Lee Allen, the first of three daughters, was born.

March 22, 1894: Ladell Allen was born. When she was a child, her name was frequently spelled "Ladelle," as is the town her father named for her in Drew County, Arkansas; however, "Ladell" is the spelling used in her obituary, on her Certificate of Death, and on her tombstone. According to the *Advance Monticellonian*, January 6, 1949, she was "known fondly by her friends as 'Dell.'"

November 26, 1895: Walter Edwin Allen was born.

August 25, 1896: Walter Edwin Allen died at the age of nine months. He was buried in Oakland Cemetery, Monticello.

November 2, 1897: Lewie Manker Allen was born.

1900: The Allen family owned its own home on North Main Street in Monticello and had a live-in servant, fifty-nine-year-old Louisa Norrill, born in Louisiana and very likely a former slave.

1905–1906: At 713 North Main Street, the original Allen House, a much smaller dwelling, was moved across the street to make room for what Joe Lee Allen hoped to be the most impressive house in town, a stunning combination of Neoclassical, Gothic, and Queen Anne styles. The large carriage house on the north side of the lot provided living quarters for servants. The architect was Chicago-trained Sylvester Hotchkiss. The builder was Josiah Barkley White.

1910: The Allens owned their new home free and clear. Lonnie Lee had completed school. The Allens had a live-in "house woman," thirty-year-old Eliza Haynes.

1912: The Allen Hotel opened.

1912: Because of his role as a significant investor, Joe Lee Allen was given the opportunity to name a new town south of Monticello. He named the new town "Ladelle," after his middle daughter.

November 29, 1914: Ladell Allen married Boyd Randolph Bonner. Boyd was born in Indiana on July 16, 1891. His draft registration card from 1917 stated that he was the owner of a "billiards hall" in Dumas, Arkansas, and was "tall" and "slender" with blue eyes and light brown hair.

April 5, 1915: Lonnie Lee Allen married Karl J. Leidinger (July 11, 1890–October 12, 1976), the son of a German immigrant. In 1910, Karl's occupation was "soda dispenser" in a drug store. In 1917, he was a "hotel keeper," probably working at the Allen Hotel. In 1917, when the United States entered World War I, Karl started spelling his name "Carl," probably in response to the widespread animosity against Americans of German ancestry. Karl entered the military on October 25, 1918, just as the war was about to end. His discharge came December 5, 1918.

November 29, 1915: Elliott Allen Bonner was born to Ladell and Boyd on their first anniversary. Boyd's father was named "Henry Elliott," but there are no references to Allen Bonner as "Elliott" even as early as the 1920 census. Newspaper stories about him referred to him as "Allen." The by-line he used on newspaper stories he wrote was "Allen Bonner." His name in his college yearbooks was "Allen Bonner." The only acknowledgement of his legal first name is his first initial on his tombstone: "E. Allen Bonner." His nickname was "Duke."

October 23, 1917: Joe Lee Allen, age fifty-four, died in Collins, Arkansas, while "demonstrating" an automobile to a potential buyer. His body was brought by friends from Collins to his house, where his funeral was held two days later. He was buried in Oakland Cemetery in Monticello.

1920: Ladell and Boyd Bonner and their son, Allen, were renters in Ft. Worth, Texas, and Boyd was operating an oil rig. In Monticello, the household at the Allen House consisted of Caddye, Lewie, Lonnie Lee, and Lonnie Lee's husband, Karl Leidinger, who paid Caddye $10 a month rent. Karl was the "proprietor of a theatre."

August 5, 1921: Karl J. Leidinger, Jr., was born to Lonnie Lee and her husband. Growing up in the Allen House, he attended public schools in Monticello and Arkansas A & M College. He went on to graduate from the medical school at the University of Arkansas at Little Rock in 1948.

October 1921: At the age of twenty-two, Lewie Allen married Robert Hale Jones, who was thirty-four. They resided in Memphis, Tennessee, and had three children: Robert, Lewis, and Martha (Ladell's only niece, who died in August 2009).

March 18, 1925: Carrie Reeves McKennon, Caddye's mother, died at the age of eighty-two.

September 1, 1927: After a marriage of nearly thirteen years, Ladell Allen Bonner was granted a divorce in Arkansas.

1930: Ladell was managing a hotel in Memphis, Tennessee, and had a "lodger," a thirty-four-year-old widow named Clide Wilson. Allen Bonner was living with his grandmother in Monticello in the Allen House, as were Lonnie Lee; her husband, Karl; and their son, Karl, Jr. Lonnie Lee's husband was the only member of the household to be listed on the census as having an occupation: "Salesman, Moving Pictures." Throughout the 1930s, the third floor of the house had the reputation among teenagers as "the party place."

1933: Mamie McKennon, Caddye's sister, died at the age of sixty-three. She was buried in Oakland Cemetery in Monticello.

1933-1935: Allen Bonner was a journalism student at Arkansas A & M College in Monticello. He wrote a humorous column called "The Lowdown" for the college newspaper, *The Southeasterner.*

1935: Allen "Duke" Bonner transferred to Baylor University. He worked as a reporter and feature writer for the *Baylor Daily Lariat*, the Baylor student newspaper.

1936: Allen Bonner was named managing editor of the *Baylor Daily Lariat*.

January 23, 1944: Allen Bonner, age twenty-eight, employed as the editor of the radio division of Associated Press, died of pneumonia at Gotham Hospital in New York City. He had lived in New York for three years and was single. He was in the hospital for ten days prior to his death. His body was transported back to Monticello, Arkansas, and he was buried at Oakland Cemetery on January 28.

September 29, 1944: Lewie Manker Allen Jones died in Memphis, Tennessee, at the age of forty-six of heart failure.

March 10, 1948: Ladell Allen Bonner and Prentiss Hemingway Savage met for the first time since a date in February 1913. They spent the day at a race track in Hot Springs, Arkansas. Prentiss made his home in Minneapolis, Minnesota, and was an executive with Texaco Oil. Within a week of their chance meeting, Prentiss initiated a correspondence that led to their love affair.

June 1, 1948: Ladell's ex-husband, Boyd R. Bonner, died in Los Angeles, California, at the age of fifty-six.

December 25, 1948: Ladell Allen Bonner consumed mercury cyanide in the master suite of the Allen House during an evening party. She was taken to the Mack Wilson Hospital less than a block away on the 26th, where she was attended by Dr. Johnnie Price.

January 2, 1949: Ladell Allen Bonner, age fifty-four, died. On the Certificate of Death, Dr. Johnnie P. Price listed the cause of death as suicide by mercury cyanide poisoning. Her funeral was held on January 4 in the Allen House and interment followed at Oakland Cemetery. Her mother, Caddye Allen, sealed off the master suite, saying she wanted to preserve it as a memorial to Ladell. The front-page announcement of Ladell's death in the January 6, 1949, edition of the *Advance Monticellonian* made no mention of the cause of death. The newspaper coverage of her death was probably reflective of the Allens' social standing and of the journalistic courtesies of the time.

July 13, 1954: Caddye Allen died at the age of eighty-three. She was buried in Oakland Cemetery. In the late 1940s, she survived a broken hip and subsequent surgery, but when she re-broke her hip in 1954, she was unable to recover.

March 9, 1955: Lonnie Lee Allen Leidinger died at the age of sixty-three. She was buried in Oakland Cemetery.

1956-1986: The Allen House, divided into apartments, became rental property owned by Joe Lee and Caddye Allen's grandson, Dr. Karl Leidinger, Jr, who lived and practiced medicine in Republic, Missouri. The property was managed by Mrs. Herschel Collins. Several tenants over the years claimed to have paranormal experiences, and by the 1970s, the house had gained a national reputation for paranormal activity.

1966: Carolyn Wilson's novel *The Scent of Lilacs*, a romantic thriller set in a mansion modeled on the Allen House, was published. Ms. Wilson and her husband lived in the Allen House in 1959.

January 21, 1985: Karl Leidinger Jr., age sixty-three, died. His widow sold the Allen House the following year. According to books, newspapers, and Internet articles, as well as a number of residents of Monticello, the new owners claimed to witness a range of paranormal activity.

1995: The house again changed owners. The new owner asserted that spirits were, indeed, present.

June 2007: The house was purchased by Mark and Rebecca Spencer.

June 7, 2008: The first "scientific" paranormal investigation of the house was to be conducted by Louisiana Spirits, but just as the team of investigators finished setting up their equipment and prepared to begin, a tree limb fell in the backyard and severed the power line to the house. The investigation was re-scheduled for June 28.

June 28, 2008: Louisiana Spirits conducted a complete paranormal investigation. In addition to the personal experiences of the team members and some provocative photographs and video, over 40 EVPs (Electronic Voice Phenomena) were recorded.

January 31, 2009: Louisiana Spirits did a follow-up investigation, capturing additional evidence of paranormal activity and new information about the identities of the entities.

June 2009: The results of an informal ballot on the website bestandworst.com ranked the Allen House the number one haunted house in America.

August 22, 2009: Mark Spencer discovered eighty-three letters hidden in the floor of the attic by Ladell Allen Bonner in 1948.

2009–2011: Paranormal investigations by various groups continued to capture not only evidence of paranormal activity but also the identities, attitudes, and moods of the spirits.

SOME NOTES ABOUT
THE LETTERS' AUTHORS

Ladell Allen Bonner: See Chronology of Facts.

Jene A. Masterman: The elderly mother of a friend of Ladell's named Mary. Ladell visited Mrs. Masterman in Stillwater, Minnesota, in August 1948. This visit was apparently the pretense for Ladell to take a trip to Minnesota to see Prentiss.

Prentiss Hemingway Savage: Born August 16, 1892, had a brother, Harry, and a sister, Genevieve. After leaving Monticello, Arkansas, in 1913, he lived in Tyler, Texas, until the start of World War I. After serving in France (1917–1918), he lived in Los Angeles and subsequently in Spokane, Washington, and then Butte, Montana, before settling in Minneapolis, where he was an executive and eventually a Vice President with Texaco Oil. He was also an executive with Ruan Transport Corporation, one of the nation's largest carriers of bulk petroleum products. His wife, Helene, was born September 3, 1895, and died July 20, 1980. She had a daughter, Jerry. Prentiss had no children. When he died in Stillwater, Minnesota, April 12, 1978, his obituary stated that his only survivors were his wife, Helene, and a niece.

Genevieve Savage Wells (1885–1965): was the sister of Prentiss Savage. She married Arthur Wells in 1905 and moved from Monticello to Helena, Arkansas, about 1925. She was aware of the relationship between her brother and Ladell and approved of it.

Frances Roddy Willa: Grew up in Monticello and was a school teacher at one time. By the 1940s she was living in Boston, Massachusetts, and spent her summers in Nova Scotia. She knew that Ladell had had a series of romantic relationships. Her first comment about Prentiss was that she couldn't help comparing him to "previous ones." She then made reference to "Hugh" and to "The Mystery Man."

Marie Wootten: Lived in Hot Springs, Arkansas, and in 1948 was instructing Ladell in Christian Science. In her letters she thanked Ladell for sending checks and then quoted passages from the Bible and from the book *Science and Health* by the founder of the Christian Science movement, Mary Baker Eddy (1821–1910).

Letters unrelated to the Savage-Bonner relationship: Found with the 1948 letters pertaining to Ladell and Prentiss' love affair were two letters from 1945. One was from Boyd Bonner, Ladell's ex-husband. Written the Sunday after Thanksgiving, the letter was chatty in recounting Boyd's Thanksgiving holiday spent with friends and acquaintances in Los Angeles, where he lived at that time. He said he would be sending Ladell a Christmas gift, and he said he hoped to see her "in the near future." He signed the letter "Love." The other 1945 letter was on stationery from the New Orleans Roosevelt Hotel and postmarked from New Orleans. The letter was heavily damaged by insects, and the writer's name was obliterated. The writer and Ladell apparently had spent some time together in New Orleans, and the writer had met Ladell's sister Lonnie and brother-in-law Karl there. He apologized if he caused Ladell trouble with Lonnie and said he regretted "Lonnie's attitude." As for Ladell, he thought she was "awfully sweet."

To Write to the Author

If you wish to contact the author or would like more information about this book, please write to the author in care of Llewellyn Worldwide Ltd. and we will forward your request. Both the author and publisher appreciate hearing from you and learning of your enjoyment of this book and how it has helped you. Llewellyn Worldwide Ltd. cannot guarantee that every letter written to the author can be answered, but all will be forwarded. Please write to:

Mark Spencer
℅ Llewellyn Worldwide
2143 Wooddale Drive
Woodbury, MN 55125-2989

Please enclose a self-addressed stamped envelope for reply, or $1.00 to cover costs. If outside the U.S.A., enclose an international postal reply coupon.